ISRAEL'S BIBLE BLOC

BY

DENNIS (AVI) LIPKIN/ALIAS VICTOR MORDECAI

1st Printing: January, 2006
Taylors, South Carolina
10,000 copies / 208 pages

Direct inquiries to:

**Dennis (Avi) Lipkin
Alias Victor Mordecai
P.O. Box 18209
Jerusalem, Israel 91181
Fax: 011 972 2 5864729
or
P.O. Box 630312
Flushing, NY 11363
Fax: 516-487-9093**

**For reordering this book in the U.S.
1-800-540-0828**

**www.vicmord.com
e-mail: vicmord2001@yahoo**

Table of Contents

Preface

In the Preface of my third and previous book, "Islamic Threat Updates Almanac #1 – 5762", I gave a brief history of how and why I wrote my first, second and third books.

The first book, "Is Fanatic Islam a Global Threat?" (1997) was written basically as a summary of my message to all people, Christians in particular, who make up almost one third of the human race, of the threat facing the world from Islamic plans for global conquest.

My second book, "Christian Revival for Israel's Survival" (1999) was written in response to what I saw as the Clinton Administration's unfair targeting of the Serbs in the Bosnia and Kosovo conflicts and "globalist" plans for subduing any and all leaders defending their nations from the Islamic threat. At that time, Ehud Barak was prime minister of Israel. But the message was that any Israeli prime minister who did not "play ball" by Washington's rules would be targeted and Israel considered just another "Serbia" to be dealt with by NATO if Israel did not withdraw from all territories taken during the self-defense wars of 1967 and 1973.

By the way, "Christian Revival" makes even more sense after the 2005 Israeli withdrawal from the Gaza Strip and part of northern Samaria and the ethnic cleansing of the Jews living in those areas. Prime Minister Ariel Sharon learned the lesson to "play ball" by Washington's rules "or else."

It was the 9/11/2001 attacks on the US that made me realize that a yearly "almanac" documenting Islamic plans for the conquest of the world was a must. I expressed my intention of indeed coming out with twelve monthly newsletters each year henceforth that would be a documentation of "evergreen" information not readily available to most people around the world. These newsletters would then be turned into hard copy book form for those good people who did not have computer/internet access.

I succeeded during that first fateful year (after the 9/11 attacks) with monthly newsletters which were then turned into my third book "Islamic Threat Updates Almanac #1 – 5762". But I was thwarted from continuing this project because of up to seven or eight months a year of traveling around the world speaking in churches, synagogues, on TV and Radio. I am still hoping to resume from where I left off with Almanac #2 – covering the period of October 2002 to September 2003 after I have published this fourth book "Israel's Bible Bloc." My apologies go out to all those people who have been waiting with patience and perseverance for Almanacs 2, 3, 4, etc. Don't despair!

The reasons for writing this fourth book "Israel's Bible Bloc" are many. The impetus for the message contained in this book came from a "prophecy" conference in March, 1998 in Springfield, Missouri sponsored by Dr. David Allen Lewis, one of Israel's best friends in the Christian world. As one of Dr. Lewis's guest speakers, I veered off my main subject of Islamic terrorism and dove directly into the need for a Judeo-Christian alliance not only in the "Bible Belt" of the US as well as in other countries around the world, but also in Jerusalem in Israel's parliament, the Knesset. The reasons will become abundantly clear in this book.

For six years, I spoke hypothetically about this idea of Christian Israelis together with Jewish Israelis marching together politically. When goaded on by Christians as to how and when this Bible Bloc Party would be created, I answered "In God's timing."

My reason for such a nebulous answer was because there was no one else (until the time of the writing of this book) and there still is no one else competing with me for the honor and burden of creating and leading such a political party. And since I had owned no home in Israel since the 1980's due to a failed business, how could I have the audacity or "chutzpa" to even consider such a venture? How can a "homeless" person who is renting in a seemingly endless way create and lead a political party? How can a person who pays taxes in the US but not in Israel be so pretentious as to consider being active in Israeli politics?

But indeed, God works in mysterious ways. It was in the summer of 2004 that all the pieces began to fit together to make up the picture of what is about to happen. We were forced out of our rented home for the last time to yet another temporary dwelling, but our new and permanent home into which we will soon be moving is nearly complete. Now we own a home in Israel. God provided that home.

Secondly, former Prime Minister and Finance Minister Benjamin Netanyahu also played a role in God's plan. He passed a reform economic bill in the Knesset that made Israelis like me who earn all their income abroad, be accountable to the Israeli IRS as well. So now, the good and bad news is that I must pay my taxes both in the US and Israel as well!

So now the road is open for me to create the "Bible Bloc Party" to run for the Knesset. I now own a home in Israel and pay taxes in Israel. So "let the show begin."

Introduction

Throughout the history of the Jewish People there have been nations and individuals who loved Israel, and then there were those who sought to eradicate the Jews. The Bible (Gen: 12:3 & Numbers 24:9) teaches us: "I will bless those who bless you and curse those who curse you." In Jewish tradition, we speak of Laban, the uncle and father-in-law of our forefather Jacob, who in his own way sought his nephew's destruction.

Within a generation, Jacob and his children descended into Egypt to sojourn there for 430 years. It was Pharaoh who enslaved our people and sought first to kill the first-born and later to drown the Children of Israel in the Red Sea. In the end, it was Egypt's first-born who perished and Pharoah's charioteers who drowned in the Red Sea. Pharaoh cursed Israel so he and his people were cursed.

In the desert, Amalek, a distant cousin, sought to destroy the stragglers in the desert, the weak, the women and the children. God commands to destroy Amalek several times in the Bible for this reason. Amalek cursed Israel so he was cursed.

In the Book of Esther, we read of Haman, who was a

descendant of Amalek, who sought our destruction, but God meted out the same punishment to Haman that Haman wished upon Mordecai and the Jews of the Persian Empire. Haman was cursed.

We see so many instances in our history of people and systems inimical to the Jews including the Inquisition in Spain, Chmielnitzky in the Ukraine in 1648 who killed a third of the Jews in the world at that time, a mini-Holocaust if you will.

Hitler was the worst case scenario with The Holocaust of 1933-1945. But it must never be forgotten that the curse of Hitler on the Jews brought about the demise of twenty million of his own German people as well. Whoever curses Israel is cursed.

But unfortunately, Jewish people seem to have a fixation with the Holocaust so great that they are blinded to other dangers even greater that the Jewish world faces today.

The problem is not one of Hitler or Nazism, but this same spirit that runs throughout history of those people who just must see Israel eliminated.

Today it is Islam that has made it clear that all Jews must die. There is no Moslem who can deny this. But the Jewish world is only now beginning to see this. It is five million Israeli Jews and another 10 million worldwide against a system controlling over one billion human beings dedicated to the destruction of Israel and all Jews in the world. The Moslems curse the Jews because the Islamic system and Allah hate the Jews. Just look at the cursed lives Moslems have throughout the Islamic world. They are the first victims of their own Islamic system. Those who curse Israel are cursed. Again this is a decision that every human must make: Either to love the Jews or to curse them and seek their destruction.

There are, believe it not, people in the world who love

the Jews because their messiah was a Jew. Whether or not Jews believe in this messiah is irrelevant. God commanded the Christians, at least the true Christians to love the Jews and stand with them. I think one of the lessons we Jews and Israelis must learn is that in light of the Holocaust, we would be remiss if we continued to ignore these friends and allies. Christians must bless the Jews, and the Christians thus must be blessed.

The question is not whether or not only Hitler and the Nazis should be remembered for the evil they did to us, but rather, should we not focus on that evil spirit from time immemorial that calls for our destruction? And should we Jews not seek to mobilize those who love us and have shown that they will stand with us in our defense?

The purpose of this book, unlike my three previous books, is to show why a Bible Bloc political party – a partnership of Jewish and Christian Israelis -- is essential for the future survival of Israel. It is also a purpose of this book to show that a Bible Bloc International based in Jerusalem, Israel, representing conservative western political parties worldwide is necessary to give backbone and strength to Judeo-Christian Western Civilization and Democracy in Israel and globally.

Whereas in my first three books, I emphasized the threat of Islam to the World, as well as the threat of Islam and its subservient, rapacious allies as a threat to Israel and the West, in this book, the emphasis will be on strengthening the bonds and kinships that Jews and Christians share, all as part of Judeo-Christian Western Civilization and Democracy. The most important bonds and kinships shared by Jews and Christians are: "Love the Lord thy God" (Deuteronomy 6:4-5) and "Love Thy Neighbor as Thyself." (Leviticus 19:18)

Professor Samuel Huntington of Harvard University

discusses in his book "The Clash of Civilizations and The Remaking of World Order" a looming crisis between the West and the East. The West, of course, is Judeo-Christian Western Civilization and Democracy led by the United States in particular. The East is comprised of Islamic, Buddhist and Hindu cultures, none of which wish to be "westernized". "Westernized" means Christianized in the eyes of the Eastern civilizations.

Huntington goes on to predict that within fifty years from now (the middle of the 21st century) the US will become a third rate power, replaced by China, India and the Islamic world. My purpose is to strengthen the US, because without the US, Israel cannot survive, Europe cannot survive, and the World cannot survive.

Much of this book will be autobiographical. The conclusions I have drawn in the 57 years of my life will be delineated through my life experiences. One of the primary conclusions of my life is that Western Democracy is a terrible system. But as Winston Churchill said, "Every other system is so much worse!"

As Jews or Christians, we all revere the Bible as God's word to the world. But it wasn't until 1863 and the Emancipation Declaration of US President Abraham Lincoln that slavery was abolished. Slavery, though frowned upon in the Bible, was an unfortunate fact to be lived with. It took the 2,000 year old synthesis of Jewish, Christian, Greek and Roman cultures to cope with and eventually to terminate once and for all, the curse of slavery in the Judeo-Christian West Women only received the vote in the United States in the 1920's because of Susan B. Anthony. Again, it was only under Judeo-Christian Western Civilization and Democracy of the United States, and later other western countries, women were finally given the vote.

But today, there are still countries primarily in the Islamic world where slavery exists. There are still countries again, primarily in the Islamic world, where women are not second class citizens but third class citizens bordering on chattel slaves.

Even in Israel, there are rabbis who teach: "Any man who walks between two women… it is as if he is walking between two donkeys." I call them the Taliban rabbis.

There are rabbis in Israel who frown on the teaching of any languages other then Hebrew and Aramaic (the language of the Talmud). Teaching of English, French, or any other foreign languages is forbidden. Learning mathematics, sciences, history, geography, etc. is forbidden. Even Bach and Beethoven are forbidden. I call them the Islamic-Taliban rabbis. They, too, must modernize and westernize.

In my first three books, I write about the threat of Islam to the World. But I have no doubt that the days of Islam are numbered if only the Jews and Christians will march united in defeating the satanic Islamic system. My concern, then, is for the future of Israel after the Islamic threat is terminated. Are we moving forward into the 21st century or are we returning to the first century?

Will Jews and Christians ever overcome their two millennia-old animosities? Will the Jews and Christians come together like never before? Is the Messiah, who we all agree is a Jew from Israel who speaks Hebrew, come to Jerusalem for only the Jews, or only the Christians? Or is Messiah coming for all of humanity? What are the steps that must be taken for this to occur? What does God want from us?

I hope to raise questions that will make the reader think. I even hope to provide some of the answers to these questions. But most important of all, I want to show the inevitability and necessity of a Judeo-Christian alliance in Jerusalem as well as globally. Please join me!

CHAPTER ONE

Love Verses Hate

In Mishna Aboth (1:12), more precisely known as Ethics of the Fathers, it says: "Hillel says: Be as the disciples of Aaron: Love peace. Pursue peace. Love your fellow human beings and bring them to the Torah!"

It almost sounds like a missionary tract. But this is what Jews are commanded to do. There is no rabbi who can disagree with these commandments. The commandments in the Mishnah/Talmud are considered almost as holy as those in the Torah. And yet I don't see the Jewish leadership or people reaching out to the Christians who share the same God, Bible and faith in a messiah who is a Jew from Israel who speaks Hebrew.

It does not say: Love peace. Pursue peace. Love your fellow JEWS. It says love your fellow human beings. This includes Christians and all other human beings.

It is here and now that I wish to begin my personal story and odyssey, so that the reader can understand how I used to hate Christians, all Christians, and how I was weaned away from the sickness of hatred. By the way, I never hated the Moslems, but always loved them, (because of certain myths and Jewish historical traditions) so much so that it blinded

1

me to certain truths that many Jews today cannot see or comprehend. I have never hated the Buddhists or Hindus, or any other human beings either for that matter. It was only the Christians I hated. Here is how I was healed.

It is not my intention to go into vain fables and genealogies. Indeed I did not know virtually anything about my forebears, going all the way back to King David, until I was about 36 years old. A cousin of mine sparked my interest in my family tree, and indeed I connected up with a Rabbi Chaim Yitzhak Lipkin of the Tel-Aviv rabbinate and he showed me where my family links up with the famous Rabbi Israel Lipkin of Salant (Lithuania). From there, rabbinical traditions link my father's family to King David.

On my mother's side, her maiden name was Kamien, based on the Slavic word for stone. Our forebears reputedly built the walls of Warsaw, Poland and were knighted by the king of Poland with the name "stone" because of the stones of the walls of Warsaw.

But because of a deterioration in the status of Jews brought about by centuries of severe Russian Czarist persecutions, my mother's and father's families in Lithuania, Ukraine, and Poland immigrated about a century ago to Buenos Aires, Argentina.

There, my mom and dad grew up as poor immigrants in Roman Catholic Argentina, the only Jews in their respective neighborhoods. All they knew was that they were Jews, though they were too poor to go to Jewish schools or synagogues to learn about their religion and too isolated from Jewish communities to know anything other than the fact they were Jews.

Indeed, both my parents were no different than their neighbors. My father even went to church as a five year old because all his friends went, and he was always with his

2

friends. Besides, his parents (my grandparents) were working too hard to feed the family to have time for my father as a child. My father, who is now 91 years old, recently surprised me by reciting the "Lord's Prayer" in Spanish. When I asked him when and where he learned this, he replied, "Ever since I was five years old when I went with my friends to church."

My mother, for her part, was raised for a time in a Catholic convent in the town of Bolivar, in the Province of Bucnos Aires, because that was the only school in the area. The nuns taught my mom only that which the state required but not the Christian classes. But my mom grew to love Johann Sebastian Bach played on the organ by the nuns. I suppose I inherited this love for Bach from my mom.

My point from all of this is that my parents' childhood experiences with their Roman Catholic neighbors in Argentina were those of love and fellowship and they never experienced anti-Semitism.

When my parents immigrated to the US in 1947 and when I was born in 1949, they decided to provide me with a Jewish/Hebrew education, something they could never have themselves in Argentina. So I started Hebrew school in New York in 1955 at age six. Obviously overshadowing my Jewish education was the Nazi Holocaust which had just ended a decade before. When I say that graduates of such a syllabus will not emerge loving German people, this is obviously an understatement. Therefore, I became an impassioned hater of the Germans. This included Austrians, Swiss and ethnically German people anywhere on the face of the Earth. For me at that time, there could not possibly be anything as a good German. Just as Nazis hated all Jews, so, too, I hated all Germans.

At the same time, Hebrew school taught us about the terrible persecutions of various Russian administrations under the Czars and later under Communism. We were taught about the infamous Cmielnitzky, the "George Washington" of the Ukraine, who, in 1648, massacred over half a million Jews in that century's equivalent of the Holocaust. We were also taught about the hatred of the Jews by Catholic Poland and Croatia. So I hated the Slavic peoples, all of them, almost as much as the Germans.

It goes without mention that I hated the Vatican and the Catholic Church for centuries of persecutions, crusades, expulsions, inquisitions, burning at the stakes, kidnapping of Jewish children, blood libels, etc. So I hated the Spanish, Portuguese, French, Italians, etc... all Catholics, almost as much as the Slavic and German nations.

Last but not least came the elitist WASPS (White Anglo-Saxon Protestants) in America who had never killed any Jews from Day 1 of American history, but with the track record of all the other Christian denominations in the world, we were taught, rest assured, that the day of Jews being massacred in America was sure to come at the hands of the WASPS as well. So I wasn't a bigot. I hated everyone.

At the same time that I hated all Christians, I had a wonderful Israeli Hebrew teacher from the town of Safed, Mr. Zvi Abbo who spent an inordinate amount of time tutoring me in Hebrew, getting me Israeli pen-pals to write to me in Hebrew, including the former first prime minister of Israel David Ben-Gurion. Zvi Abbo taught me about Zionism and sparked my interest in moving to Israel.

Indeed it was Ben-Gurion who wrote to me when I was 15 explaining that all Jews must return to the Land of Israel. It is prophetic. It is biblical. And any Jew who does not immigrate to Israel will see his children intermarry with Christians and disappear from Jewish history. Since I didn't like Christians, and I definitely did not want my progeny to

4

marry them, so at the ripe age of 15, I decided the day would come soon that I would move to Israel.

By age 16, I joined the Betar (Brit Yosef Trumpeldor/ Riga) Youth Movement and became a "Blue Shirt". The Mussolini youth had black shirts. The Nazi youth had brown shirts. And I wore the Jewish blue shirt. We did not consider ourselves fascist in the negative sense, as we viewed the Italian and German models. But we definitely considered ourselves to be nationalistic Jews "en route" to Israel. For me, it was always "Israel Uber Alles." My people Israel came first, last and always, exclusively.

At age 19, I finally moved to Israel after my sophomore year at New York University, Washington Square College, as part of the Junior Year Abroad Program of Hebrew University in Jerusalem, Israel. And it was at Hebrew University that I completed my BA majoring in Sovietology and with a minor in Spanish and Latin American studies in 1973. Interestingly, one of the most important conclusions I drew from my Russian and Spanish studies was the common denominator: Underlying the development of these two cultures was a millennia of war with Islam.

It was also at Hebrew University that I met my bride-to-be, Racheline Romy, a recently arrived immigrant from Egypt. God has a sense of humor, and indeed, I have to thank Betar for our meeting. I had just gotten onto the #9 bus from Jerusalem's city-center en route to the Givat Ram campus wearing my Betar uniform. I had just participated in an official Betar function and so I got on the bus innocently enough and immediately began to hear some pretty nasty remarks behind my shoulder by some recent "Bolshevik" immigrants from Argentina, Uruguay and Chile who had just escaped death in their home countries at the hands of the fascist military dictatorships they had just fled. It was

5

January 14th, 1970.

Since Latin American curses usually involve the mother of the person being cursed, and since I understood every word, I turned on them and began haranguing them in Spanish (my mother tongue). But like I said, God has a sense of humor. My eyes fell on Rachel, my wife to be, who was studying with these young communist activists. She bore the brunt of my wrath. She had just left Hebrew ulpan classes with them, went shopping at the supermarket with them, and then was innocently standing alongside them on the bus carrying shopping bags full of food.

Ironically, my eyes fell on her. My Spanish language tirade was directed at her, at which time, she calmly told me that she wasn't from Argentina and didn't speak Spanish. So I felt like a fool and immediately apologized for picking on the wrong person.

God has a sense of humor. From that moment on, I disregarded my defamers, and focused all my attentions on Rachel. She told me she was from Egypt. She had just arrived three weeks before as a new immigrant.

Since I was the editor of the English language Hebrew University newspaper "Golem", I found a scoop! I thought it remarkable that Jewish people were coming home to Israel from Egypt. Could I interview her, I asked? She said yes. So I dutifully carried her shopping bags from bus #9 to her campus dormitory room and two years later, we married! (By the way, Israeli army censorship did not allow me to publish the interview because it could threaten other people still in Egypt seeking to leave.)

In our first real, serious conversation, the first thing Rachel asked/said to me: "Are you crazy? Why did you leave America? America was rich. Israel was poor. America was at peace. Israel was at war. Why did you leave your mom and

6

dad to come to live in Israel?"

My answer was two-fold. Firstly, I said to her, "I am a Zionist. Ben-Gurion told me to come home to Israel. So I came home. Besides," I said, "The Goyim (gentiles) hate us!"

Rachel, very incredulously asked, "The Goyim? And who might the Goyim be?"

"The Christians," I answered. After all, in America, if one is not a Jew, one is a Goy. And in America, whoever is not a Jew is a Christian. Therefore, Christian = Goy.

In a very non-chalant manner, my wife countered, "Oh, you don't know anything!"

Christians cannot be "goyim", Rachel said. In Egypt, the Jews and Christians are considered one people, "The People of the Book." The Arabic term for this is Ahel al-Kitab. We have the same God, the God of Abraham, Isaac and Jacob. We have the same Bible, and we all believe in a messiah who is a Jew from Israel who speaks Hebrew. The only difference between Jews and Christians, she said, is that Jews keep the Sabbath on Saturday, and Christians keep the Sabbath on Sunday.

The Moslems, now, they are the goyim. They have a different god, Allah, a pagan moon-god, war-god and sword-god. They have a different book, the Koran, which replaces and destroys the Bible of the Jews and Christians. And for the Moslems, the Moslem messiah is coming to kill the Jews on Saturday and the Christians on Sunday.

Now, of course, I was shocked to hear this from Rachel, because for the first twenty years of my life, I hated Christians and loved the Moslems. This was a rude awakening for me. I was so influenced by the movie "Lawrence of Arabia" that my mother used to call me "Avi of the Negev" (a desert in the south of Israel). I loved the Arabs. I saw them as

7

perpetual allies of the Jews in the face of two millennia of Christian persecution (as do most Jews today). In fact, one of the reasons I fell in love with Rachel and married her was her Arabic culture. She spoke Arabic, as did her parents, siblings and friends. I loved her Middle Eastern cuisine. She helped to teach me Arabic, listen to Arabic music and watch Egyptian movies.

How could she do something like that? How could she shatter my illusions that the Moslems were the allies and the Christians the enemies? Illusions I had held for the first two decades of my life?

Now, I always listen to Rachel. But in this case, it took me seventeen years before I began to understand what she was saying. I am fortunate Rachel has had 35 years of patience with me until "things sink in!"

Indeed, seventeen years later in 1986, I started corresponding with Nancy from Texas. I received her name through Ray and Sharon Sanders of Christian Friends of Israel, a humanitarian organization providing food, clothes, eyeglasses and other articles to the needy of Israel. They had placed an advertisement in the Jerusalem Post, Israel's English language daily, looking for English speaking Israeli pen-pals for American Christian Zionists. This aroused my curiosity. How could Christians be Zionists?

After a few exchanges of letters, I was pleasantly shocked to find a Christian who loved Israel and Jews. When I was illegally fired from the Prime Minister's Office in October 1990, and found it impossible to get a job appropriate to my qualifications in Israel, it was Nancy who opened the doors for me in churches, synagogues, radio and TV in Texas.

In November 1990, I attended a Christian church service for the first time in my life. I was almost 41 years old and was shocked at what I saw. I saw people fainting, falling to the ground, "speaking in tongues", and just doing things Jews are not used to seeing. It was known as a "spirit-filled" church: Tree of Life Fellowship in New Braunfels, Texas.

Pastor Don Duncan gave an impassioned sermon about how Christians needed to love Israel and love the Jews. Now I knew why Nancy loved Israel and the Jews. The whole church was like that. And in the last 16 years, I have spoken in over 400 of these churches around the world.

My next surprise was to see how many ethnic Germans attended that church in what is known as the "New Bavaria" of Texas. I hated Germans, as aforementioned, but these American Germans cried tears of love and repentance for Israel and the Jews, so I came to the conclusion that these German-Americans were OK Germans. They were kosher! I could not hate these Germans any more.

In January 1996, I was invited by Jan Willem van der Hoeven of the International Christian Embassy of Jerusalem to make a presentation at the Third International Zionist Christian Congress in Jerusalem. I was to screen the PBS video "Jihad In America" with a brief speech introducing the video, which had been shown on American and Israeli TV in November 1994. This video was prophetic and predicted the 9/11 attacks destroying aircraft and the World Trade Center Towers in New York. But because the "Jihad In America" was "politically incorrect" it was suppressed by the "liberal" agenda under pressure from the Moslems.

At the end of my presentation, two clearly looking European intellectuals came up to me and speaking in a heavy German accent, invited me to come to speak at their pastors' seminary. My first response in my heart was: "I am not stepping on German soil."

When they said their seminar was in Basel, Switzerland, I started to stretch myself, thinking that Switzerland was neutral in WWII and maybe, maybe I should go. So I went.

I had the honor of speaking before about 5,000 German speaking people along with other speakers such as Ludwig Schneider of the German Israeli monthly news magazine "Nachrichten Aus Israel." ("News from Israel"). It was the same hall in which Theodore Herzl, the founder of Zionism spoke in 1897, exactly a century before.

The people in the audience, like those in New Braunfels, Texas cried tears of love for Israel and the Jews as well as repentance for the Holocaust and past sins against the Jews. I thought to myself: These Swiss Germans are different than the German and Austrian Germans. So they must be kosher also, just like the American Germans in New Braunfels.

But at the reception, when I asked them what part of Switzerland they were from, they answered: Nein, Deutschland! Or Nein, Osterreich. (No, we are from Germany or Austria). So I realized that there were good Germans in Germany and Austria as well as from Switzerland. They were kosher too! I was having the scales of hatred removed from my eyes.

And here is how the last scale of hatred was removed from my eyes. Ludwig Schneider of Nachrichten Aus Israel said that my first book "Is Fanatic Islam a Global Threat?" should be translated into German. I answered by saying that his magazine should be published in English. After two years, the German magazine started finally to come out in English: Israel Today. And I am the co-founder with Ludwig and his son Aviel Schneider. By the way, this magazine also appears in Japanese now!

But getting back to my first book, "Fanatic Islam" I told Schneider to go ahead and publish the book in German. He said, "No, you must do this with a German publisher." But I answered him that I "hated" Germans and Germany and would not do any business with them.

He said, "Listen, Haenssler-Verlag is a Zionist, Christian German publisher. When the Nazis came to power in Germany in 1933, his church hymnal publishing firm was shut down when it refused to delete Israel or Zion from the church hymnals. Then during WWII, Friedrich Haenssler, who was sixteen years old at the time was mobilized into the Wehrmacht and sent to the Russian Front, a virtual death sentence.

During his service in the Ukraine, Friedrich Haenssler was one day called upon to pick up his gun and "go shooting in the forest." For him, he thought it was hunting for wild game to supplement their rations. But when he came to a clearing in the forest and saw the naked Jewish women, children and old people being lined up and shot into trenches, and he was to be in the next firing squad, Friedrich looked up into the heavens and said, "Jesus Christ, if you are really there, please don't let me kill the Jews."

At that point, the firing squad commander called out, "Haenssler, Raus!" or Haenssler, out of the firing line. And he never killed one Jew in WWII.

So I decided. Haenssler-Verlag would publish my book. Something inside of me broke. There were good Germans. There were Christian Germans. There were Zionist Germans. And I loved them. I could not hate them anymore. I would fight Nazism to my last breath, but German people are not necessarily bad and are probably people no different than any others.

Interestingly, suppressed in the back recesses of my mind was a mention made by my maternal grandfather that in 1914, during WWI, the Germans entered Warsaw, Poland as liberators of the Jews. It was the Czarist Russian administration that was "ethnically cleansing" and persecuting the Jews. It was the aristocratic, cultured and refined German/Prussian officers who fed, clothed and provided for my family and for the Jews of Warsaw. They spoke German. We spoke Yiddish. So we understood each other and had an excellent rapport with the German soldiers.

This fact may help to explain how six million Jews allowed themselves to be shipped off to their deaths in the Holocaust in WWII. Nobody could believe the metamorphosis that had taken place in the heart of the Germans under the Nazi regime. The Germans went from being the kindest and friendliest of nations to the Jews in WWI to the meanest and cruelest under Hitler.

And if I didn't hate the Germans, how could I hate the Russians? True, the Czarists persecuted us, as did the Russian Orthodox Church. Later Communism slaughtered and enslaved us as it did the Russian people. But I could not hate the people any more. I would fight Communism to my last breath, this evil anti-Semitic, anti-Christian and anti-human system, but the Russian people were good people, just like any other nation.

And thus, I could not hate the Catholics any more. Sure, there were many aspects of the Vatican and Catholic Church history that are too painful to remember, but Catholic people are good people just like any others. At the same time, the Catholic Church as a result of the Nostra Aetate of 1965, renounced the teaching that the Jews killed Christ, thus following the lead of the Protestant churches which dropped that teaching centuries ago. And indeed, the Vatican corrected an anomaly by finally establishing diplomatic relations with Israel in 1991, the last European government to do so.

By the way, at this point, it is important to say a few words about the Protestants. Most Jews, whether they be American, Israeli, or otherwise know very little about the Protestant

Reformation and the Wars of Reformation with the Catholic Church. Indeed, following the invention of the printing press, came the printing of the Bible in such massive quantities that now, any Christian could go directly to the Bible for guidance from God. Bibles were no longer hand-written manuscripts available only to the richest. Anyone could now own a Bible. There was no more need for an intermediary priest. It was at this time that the corruption in the Catholic Church led to breakaway Protestant denominations. And these Bible believing Protestants were severely persecuted by the Catholic Church.

Most Jews do not know that Protestants were burned at the stake alongside the Jews in the auto-da-fe of the Catholic Church. It was the Protestant Oliver Cromwell who invited the Jews back into England four centuries after they were expelled by the Catholics during the Expulsion of York. It was Holland and Belgium that gave asylum to the "Marranos" or Jews decades after they were forcibly converted to Catholicism in Spain and Portugal in 1492-3. The Jews were allowed to return to Judaism and live peacefully in Holland and Belgium under the Protestants.

It was the United States and the British colonies all over the world that allowed the Jews to immigrate to their shores and blessed the Jews, and never ever killed them as happened in Europe and in Islamic countries.

But again, most Jews in America know pitifully little about the Protestants and lump them together with the Catholics. The same applies to many people, including and especially rabbis in Israel who have never read the New Testament, know nothing about the development of Christianity and therefore, cannot understand why true Christians love us.

So concluding Chapter I, I must say, I don't hate the Germans, the Slavic nations, the Catholics or the Protestants any more. I have been healed of that hatred. I only have love for Christians, Hindus, Buddhists, and I have ALWAYS loved the Moslems. Remember Avi of the Negev!

But I will fight the perverted systems which threaten the annihilation of my people, especially, Nazism, Communism and Islam. In the next chapter, the Five Deceptions of Islam, I will show how Moslems are good people, but their system is anti-Semitic (anti-Jewish) and anti-Christian.

And just as the Germans were good to the Jews in 1914, so were the Moslems better to the Jews than the Christians in Spain of 1492, but we see later, the madness that took over in Nazi Germany as well as the madness of Islam in the 20th-21st century.

The lesson should not be lost. The Moslems were our allies in Spain in 1492, but today, Islam seeks the death of all Jews and the wiping of Israel off the face of the Earth. Yet intelligent Jews continue to prefer the Moslem enemies over the Christian Bible believing allies because of the memories of 1492. Jews refuse to accept that there has been a metamorphosis in the Islamic approach to Israel and Jews in the last 100 years. This refusal could lead, God-forbid, to a new catastrophe, an Islamic Holocaust of the Jews worse than anything we have seen in our 4,000-year history.

Conversely, as a result of the Protestant Reformation, there has been a metamorphosis of Bible believing Christians who now love the Jews after 1,500 years of hatred engendered by the Roman Catholic and Greek Orthodox churches. The Moslem allies of the past are now the mortal enemies. The Christians, our mortal enemies of the past are now our allies without whom we will not survive. Even the Catholic Church has stopped teaching hate against the Jews over the last 40 years. Hopefully, one day soon, so will the Eastern Orthodox churches stop teaching that the Jews killed Jesus,

14

and become our allies.

And just as Christians need to overcome their hatred of us, so too, do Jews need to grow up! We need to get over it! We must stop driving our car with our eyes on the rear-view mirror and look ahead otherwise we will inevitably crash. We must stop focusing on Holocausts past and prepare for and prevent Holocausts just about to happen!

Chapter II will outline why Islam is so dangerous to the Jews, the Christians and to all humanity, and the Holocaust it is preparing for all of us, including the Moslems themselves.

CHAPTER TWO

The Five Deceptions of Islam

As I concluded in the previous chapter, there is a mindset amongst most Jews that makes Jews prefer Moslems over Christians when the choice must be made. It is undeniable that the Islamic world was slightly more benevolent to the Jews than the Christian world during the first centuries of Islam. Jews fled from Christian lands to Moslem lands, or were overtaken by the Islamic invasions of Christian lands, and as long as the Jews agreed to become "dhimmis" or second-class subservient subjects, they were tolerated in Islamic lands. Indeed, it was often the case that Jews would become prominent in Islamic administrations and the court. There was an immediate, albeit, temporary need in the Islamic world for Jews (and Christians), the People of the Book, who knew how to read and write and help run the Islamic empire since the Islamic conquerors were, by and large, illiterate desert nomads. But the day would come when these illiterate desert nomads would no longer be illiterate. The Jews and Christians would then have to convert or pay the "Jiziyah". And eventually, the whole world would become Moslem until there would be no more Jews or Christians.

The fact is that the onerous head tax known in Arabic as

17

the "Jiziyah" paid by Jews and Christians but not by Moslems was a cause for conversion to Islam. It is also known that every so often, Islamic leaders would decide not to be so tolerant of the Jews and Christians and "make them an offer they couldn't refuse." Hence, entire Jewish and Christian communities were forced to convert to Islam, leave the empire or be put to the sword. A famous example of this, the famous Jewish philosopher and physician, Maimonides, who had to flee one fanatic Islamic country Spain, to go to Morocco, where Moslems claim he converted to Islam, (Jews say forcibly) and then fled Morocco to the Holy Land, and then finally settled for the rest of his life in Egypt and became personal physician to the king. All these countries were Islamic with varying degrees of fanaticism interspersed with tolerance in their leaders.

Indeed, it was Maimonides who said in his writings that it was permissible for Jews to pray inside of mosques, but not churches, because according to Maimonides, the churches were pagan houses of worship. This is a common theme in the Talmud. And indeed, this is one of the reasons that many religious Jewish people will speak in a church but not in the sanctuary in front of a cross. It is also a reason for the fallacy that we are closer to the Moslems than to the Christians.

On the other hand, Maimonides was also quoted as saying that it is permissible for a Jew to teach a Christian the Torah because the Christian revered the Torah. But it was not permissible to teach a Moslem the Torah, because the Islamic Koran replaced and destroyed the Torah according to Islamic belief. And for that reason, I will speak in any church, even in the sanctuary, and even if there is a cross.

Conversion to Islam or Christianity was always a reality faced by the Jewish minorities scattered throughout the world. That perhaps explains why there are so few Jews

18

today in the world, and why there are so many Moslems and Christians who can claim Jewish blood in their veins and arteries. Besides, right or wrong, it is a Jewish tradition to frown on non-Jews converting to Judaism because in the Talmud it says that converts are like scabs that never really become Jews. Tell that to Ruth and Naomi. Also after the failed Bar Kochba revolt of 132-135 AD (CE) the Romans made teaching the Torah to anyone a capital crime especially the conversion of non-Jews to Judaism. Indeed, it is an historical fact that 10% of the Roman Empire was Jewish at some time.

After Constantine adopted Christianity as the state religion of the Roman Empire, the decree forbidding Jewish proselytizing was continued under the Church. Judaism was not allowed to proselytize. Only Christianity could. When Islam came to the fore, it adopted the same rules.

And so, between the Talmud's teaching that converts are scabs, and the rule by the Christians and Moslems forbidding the Jews from proselytizing, the rabbis became very comfortable with seeing the Jewish world as a small, cliquish, elitist religion, whereas Moslems and Christians are only too happy to welcome Jewish converts, forced or otherwise.

Another reason for Jews to prefer Islam as a system over Christianity is the latter's faith in Jesus of Nazareth as God, the Son of God, or the Messiah, as well as faith in the Trinity. Jews and Moslems are in agreement theologically in their opposition to any of these.

So, what do the Jews and Christians share in common? In the end, are the Jews closer to the Christians or to the Moslems? This debate will heat up very soon as the Bible Bloc Party gets elected to the Knesset and the Judeo-Christian alliance solidifies.

This will force Jewish people to rethink history both in Israel as well as globally. There will have to be quantum leaps in Jewish thinking. The Jewish People will have to emerge from two thousand years of thinking that is no longer valid, to emerge from the jail cells of the Diasporas and to return home to the Land of Israel, our home past, present and future.

So what are the Five Deceptions of Islam that have the World so fooled?

Islam is a religion of love.

Islam is a religion of peace.

Allah is God.

Jesus of Islam is the same as Jesus of Christianity.

The Koran is divine, infallible word of Allah to Mohammed.

DECEPTION NUMBER 1

Is Islam a Religion of Love?

Does Islam command its believers to love as the Bible commands Jews and Christians? "Love the Lord Thy God" (Deuteronomy 6:4-5) and "Love Thy Fellow as Thyself" (Leviticus 19:18) are indeed a commonality for Jews and Christians. This is confirmed and reinforced for the Christians in the New Testament. In fact these two commandments are the most important of all for Christians. In my opinion, the Judeo-Christian belief is a system of love, the God of Abraham, Isaac, and Jacob is a God of love and the Bible can be distilled into a four letter word: love.

And yet, these two commandments are absent in the Koran and the Hadith (an Islamic teaching based on sayings or traditions of Mohammed, yet not included in the Koran).

If these two commandments are absent in Islamic commandments, how can Islam be a religion of love?

20

So why are Moslems loving people just as any other people? The answer is simple. Moslems just like any other people are created in the image of God. According to the Judeo-Christian understanding of God, people can have a loving relationship with the Father in Heaven. If our God is a loving God and we are in His image, so it reasons that we are creations of love.

But nowhere in the Koran or the Hadith are Moslems taught to have a loving relationship with Allah. Allah is to be feared not loved. One cannot love Allah. It is like can one love Zeus (of the ancient Greek pagan gods)? We will talk about the pagan origins of Allah momentarily.

I used to hate Germans. I thought they were all evil. But now I see Germans are like any other people. Germans are also in the image of God. They are capable of loving and can be good people just like any others. But Nazis are evil and are taught to hate.

Nazism is an evil system. And Nazism is anti-Semitic, anti-Christian and anti-human. Nazism helped to bring about the deaths of over 70 million people in WWII, including 20 million Germans.

I used to hate Russians. But just like the Germans, Russians are also good people and loving people because they, too, are in the image of God. But Communists are taught to hate because Communism is an evil system. It is also anti-Semitic, anti-Christian, and anti-human. Communism killed at least one million Jews and 40 million Christians. In Cambodia, the Khmer Rouge regime under Pol Pot killed 2 million Cambodians. And only God knows how many people died in China and North Korea under the Communist system.

Similarly, my conclusion is that Moslems are good people like any other people, but their system is devoid of the two most important commandments: Love the Lord Thy God and Love Thy Fellow as Thyself. And Islam is an evil system. It is anti-Semitic, anti-Christian, anti-human and you know what? Islam is even anti-Moslem. We will also review examples of this shortly.

Slightly changing the subject, I would like to share some thoughts as a grandfather and try to put myself in God's shoes for a moment.

When parents have children, invariably both parents like to find similarities in the child that has just been born. Does he/she more resemble the father or the mother? Even if the parents are madly in love with each other, usually, the mom or the dad wishes the child to resemble the mom more or the dad more depending on the case. In fact some parents wish their children were clones!

The reason for this is that we are in the image of our biological parents who created us. I will never forget when Rachel and I married and had children, one of the first reactions clearly was: "Does he resemble me or Rachel?" Parents are very jealous and wish that the children resemble the parents. And so, God sees us, all his children, as resembling Him. God is also very jealous of all his children, because we are all in his image.

God blessed us with two sons, Aaron and Jacob. Well, Aaron resembles me, but has his mom's green eyes. Jacob resembles is mom but has my blue eyes. So do you know what God is saying? When you marry, you must share the genes! And then the children are in the image of both mother and father.

Next Generation: My two sons marry. Aaron, the elder, marries a beautiful dark-skinned girl with whom he served in the army. She is half Yemenite and half-Algerian in background. Esther is strikingly beautiful, but I knew one thing. Her children would not be blond and blue eyes like my family. Now I was never a racist, but I wanted grandchildren who would be my clones! I wanted them in my image.

And the fact is my grandchildren on Aaron's side don't resemble me at all, but I love them with all my heart. They drive me crazy and I drive them crazier. After all, they are in my image. They are my flesh and blood.

When Jacob married, his wife Dana was the daughter of Russian immigrants to Israel. She had brown hair and brown eyes, also beautiful. But I had that feeling that none of my grandchildren would ever have blue eyes like I had. When their daughter was born, we were all surprised to find a Scandinavian princess: blond and blue eyes.

All of sudden it clicked. Now I had three chocolates and one vanilla! I love chocolate ice cream. I love vanilla ice cream. But most important of all I love "swirl". And I love to swirl with all my grandchildren all at the same time. Had I two more sons, I would be perfectly content if they married banana and strawberry!

And indeed I think God is a "Baskin-Robbins 31 Flavors" God. (Baskin-Robbins is a famous American ice cream company known for its 31 flavors) He loves all his children in the world regardless of their skin color, racial, or ethnic background. God is completely color-blind. All humans are His children. We are all in God's image.

What does God want from us? God wants us to love Him. What do parents want from their children? All they want is love in return for the blessings God and parents bestow on their children. Hence the commandment: Love the Lord Thy God.

What makes God and parents unhappy? Unhappiness for parents is when children do not love them. Similarly, unhappiness for God is when we do not love Him.

What makes God and parents happy? When children love each other, grow up together, and bless each other. What makes God and parents unhappy? When children hate each other, curse each and kill and torment each other. The worst thing for a parent is to see the fruit of the womb – the children hating each other. The worst thing for a parent is to bury a child. The same applies to God. The worst thing for God is when any of His children die before him, or go hungry, or suffer, or are tortured in His name.

This is the kind of God-inspired system and civilization we live in under the Judeo-Christian way. All human beings are created in the image of God and are to love God and be loved by God.

DECEPTION NUMBER 2:

Is Islam a religion of Peace?

Now, let us link up with Islam's second deception: That it is a religion of peace.

Islam claims it is a religion of peace because the word Islam comes from the word Salaam which means peace. But that is kind of like saying pacification comes from the word peace, so pacification means peace. In the Viet Nam war, pacification usually meant that some Viet Cong village was immolated in napalm.

Pacification means the forced conquest, rendition or destruction of the enemy. It does not mean peace. This is what Islam really means.

Islam clearly defines the world as being divided into two: the Dar es-Salaam and Dar el-Harb. Dar es-Salaam or House of Peace is the House of Islam. Dar el-Harb or House of War is the House of the infidel, (anyone not a Moslem).

There will not be peace on Earth until the Dar es-Salaam vanquishes the Dar-el-Harb. In other words, there will not be peace until there are no more Jews, Christians, Hindus, Buddhists, Blacks, pagans, atheists, and even some Moslems are considered infidels, too. They must be destroyed as well.

Allow me to provide you with a sampling of the Islamic utopia House of Peace:

Firstly will be Afghanistan. Afghanistan used to be a country of Hindus and Buddhists. Then came the Judeo-Christians and everyone got along fine. Then came the Moslems.

The first to be destroyed were the pagans: the Hindus and Buddhists. The Jews and Christians are respected by the Moslems (sic). We, together, are the People of the Book or Ahel al-Kitab. So we were destroyed next.

Once everyone else was destroyed and only Moslems remained, then the Moslems destroyed each other. There are four groups in Afghanistan: Pashtuns, Uzbeks, Tadjiks, and Hazaras. They are all Moslems, and they are all fighting each other to the finish.

The country self-destructs, and everyone is angry with the US and the West for not coming in more quickly to rebuild the mess Islam has created.

The second example is Iraq's Saddam Hussein. Saddam did not kill Hindus, Buddhist, Jews or Christians. He killed Moslems, mostly Shi'ites, but he also killed Sunnis, Kurds, Kuwaitis and even his own family members. Some people estimate Saddam killed up to 2 million people, all Moslems. US President George W. Bush is to be commended for delivering Iraq and the Middle East of the Saddam Hussein scourge.

The third example is Algeria. Here is a country that has no Hindus, Buddhists, Jews or Christians. There are even no Shi'ite Moslems. All Algerians are Sunni Moslems and all are ethnically homogeneous. But there is a civil war. The military government canceled democratic elections which the Moslem radicals won. Since then, over the last eight years, 200,000 Algerians have been killed by fellow Algerians.

Let me tell you a story. My wife, Rachel, monitors Al-Jazeera as part of her job for Israel Radio's Arabic Language Monitoring Department. Al-Jazeera recently interviewed a fanatic Algerian Moslem who had been captured by the less religiously Moslem military.

He explains the modus operandi of his terrorist gang. Such and such a village in the Algerian mountains is considered to be a traitorous village (cooperating with the more secular military government.) It is decided the village must be annihilated. So the terrorists reconnoiter the village and notice that by 6am daily, the men are all gone on their way to work in the city.

The terrorists then close in on the village, which now has only defenseless women, children and elderly. They demand and receive a festive meal, then pop hallucinatory pills which get the terrorists on a high. Then they rape the women, slit their throats, and then go on to slit the throats of the children and elderly till no one is left alive.

But it is not yet over. Then they go to their pickup trucks, pull out chain saws and dismember the bodies of their arms and legs. Why? Because it says in the Koran Sura V verse 33: "Any one who makes war against Allah and Mohammed and spreads disorder in the land, we will kill, we will crucify. We will chop their arms and legs off on alternate sides. And we will banish them from the Earth."

And this is what Moslems do to Moslems. This war in Algeria has nothing to do with Jews, Christians, Hindus, Buddhists, or even Shi'ite Moslems. It has nothing to do with Israel. This is simply slaughter for the sake of slaughter in the name of Allah. And so indeed, Islam is an anti-Moslem system. It kills its own people.

Again, it cannot be emphasized enough that chopping off arms and legs is not only accepted in Islam. It is a commandment. What does Judaism say? The opposite!!! In the Biblical conception, the blood is identified with life (Deut. 12:23) 'for the blood is life.' This thought was the obvious deduction from the fact that as the blood is drained from the body, the vitality weakens until it ceases altogether. Life, in every form, has in it an element of holiness, since God is the source of all life.

Therefore, although permission was given to eat the flesh of an animal, this was done with one special restriction, that life must altogether have departed from the animal before man partakes of its flesh.

According to the great Jewish sage Rashi, the restriction was of a twofold nature. It firstly forbade cutting a limb from a live animal – a barbarous practice common among primitive races; and secondly, the blood must not on any account be eaten, since it was the seat of life. This double prohibition, of cruelty to animals and the partaking of blood, is the basis of most of the rules of Jewish slaughter of animals (Shechitah) and of the preparation (koshering) of meats, which have been observed by Jews from time immemorial. (From the Pentateuch and Haftorahs, Soncino Press, London p. 32).

In fact, Moslems call Islam "Din e-Sif" or religion of the sword. You can see the sword on the flag of Saudi Arabia. In Sura II verse 216 it says in English: "Fighting is obligatory for you, much as you dislike it. But you may hate a thing although it is good for you, and love a thing although it is bad for you. Allah knows, but you know not."

Now is fighting a bad thing? Not necessarily. For those acquainted with the American tradition, fighting can be a good thing sometimes. I'll never forget my 12th grade history teacher in New York, Judson Lincoln. He used to quote Alexis de Tocqueville, author of "Democracy in America" as saying, "In America, we fight for our democracy!" Americans fight for democracy. Americans fight for freedom, etc.

But the way the Koran is translated hides what it really says in the original Arabic. The same verse when correctly translated: "Slaughtering people (with the sword) is obligatory for you, much as you dislike it. But you may hate a thing although it is good for you (slaughtering people with the sword), and love a thing although it is bad for you. Allah knows, but you know not."

Is the religion of the Jews and Christians a religion of the sword? For Jews and Christians, the sword is something defiling and detestable. And yet, the sword is one of the symbols of Islam. It must never be forgotten that Allah's origins are in the pagan moon god "AL-ILAHI", the war god, and the sword god. And again, the Moslems are proud of their religion of the sword.

In Genesis 9 verse 6, it says: "Anyone who sheds the blood of a fellow human being will have his blood shed because human beings are created in the image of God." This sounds like the opposite of Islam.

It says many times in the Bible, that when the Israelites were building an altar or temple that no iron implements could be used because iron was an implement of death, the death of human beings created in God's image. The sword was of iron.

Jews and Christians love King David, but King David was disqualified from building the Temple in Jerusalem because he was a man of the sword. King David had blood on his hands. King David killed human beings.

So it was King Solomon who built the Temple. He made

28

love not war! His sins were numerous like all human beings, but he did not shed blood.

So far, we can see the Jewish approach. What do Christians share in common with the Jews? When Peter sliced off the ear of the Roman legionnaire, Jesus said to him: "Put the sword away. He who lives by the sword dies by the sword."

Contemporary with the Christian New Testament is Pirkei Avot, or The Ethics of the Fathers, a Jewish form of post-Biblical philosophy. In chapter 2 verse 7, it says (Hillel) saw a skull floating on the water; he said to it: 'Because you drowned others, they drowned you; and those who drowned you will be drowned eventually." Again, he who lives by the sword dies by the sword.

So much for Islam being a religion of peace. But is Islam really a religion at all? There is a joke which goes like this: What is the difference between neurotic people and psychotic people?

Answer: Neurotic people dream about castles in the air. Psychotic people live in castles in the air.

Now, Adolph Hitler was psychotic for many reasons. I will share only two of them. He thought he could conquer the Earth. And secondly, he thought he could wipe all the Jews off the face of the Earth. Why are these two ideas psychoses?

Firstly, no one person or system can conquer the Earth. Alexander the Great tried it. The Romans, Napoleon, Hitler and Stalin all tried it and failed. Anyone who thinks he can conquer the Earth then is psychotic or living in castles in the air. Only the Lord has dominion over all the Earth.

Secondly, no one person or system can wipe all the Jews off the face of the Earth.

For those who believe in God, and His word, the Bible, it says in Jeremiah: "There will be no more Jews on the face of the Earth when the moon, the sun and the stars no longer shine." What this means for Bible believers is that we all had better pray for the Jews because when they're gone, the world will be gone!

But for those who do not believe in God, everyone knows the Jews have been scattered all over the world. If a man or system cannot conquer the Earth, then neither can he or it reach all the Jews to kill them. Anyone who believes to the contrary is psychotic... living in castles in the air.

What does Islam believe? Firstly, Islam plans to conquer the world. This is psychosis #1, just as crazy as Hitler.

Secondly, Islam's final plans include the "Final Solution" or annihilation of all the Jews on the face of the Earth. This is psychosis #2. Until now, Islam is just as crazy as Hitler's Nazism.

But even worse are the following psychoses. Unlike Hitler, Islam must also annihilate all the Christians who refuse to convert to Islam. (First we kill the Jews on Saturday. Then we kill the Christians on Sunday – a famous Moslem saying.) Hitler indeed did kill Christians as well as Jews, but it was not his intended, stated purpose. And the Christians make up one third of the world's population. This is psychosis #III.

And of course, the pagans have to go. The Hindus are about 1 billion, psychosis #4. And the Buddhists are also pagans. They are about 2 billion, psychosis #5.

Psychosis #6 is that one billion, or thereabouts, Moslems will annihilate 5 billion non-Moslems. Now, that is really living in castles in the air.

So Islam, indeed, is not a religion, but a psychosis. Islam is a sickness. But I believe we are to love even and especially the sick. These Moslems must be prayed for and led away from their satanic system, Islam, just as someone who is mentally ill must be helped to heal from that mental illness. Since the Jewish rabbinic leadership does not believe in missionary work to the Moslems, and since it is only the Christians who teach the Bible worldwide, I encourage the Christians to "Bring the Moslems to the Lord or they will bring all of us to the sword."

Following this is another joke about mental illness which I believe is applicable to Islam. I honor former Israel Member of Knesset Elyakim Ha'etzni who told me this joke.

It seems there is this very talented, and handsome young high school graduate. His grades in school were very good, and he was well liked by his peers. He had only one problem: a slingshot.

This young lad had only one thing on his mind: breaking every window in town with his slingshot. Now, obviously, the elders of the town in which he lived realized that such a man was a danger to his surroundings in spite of his good grades and friendliness to others. And so he was hospitalized in a mental institution hoping that something could be done to dissuade him from breaking every window in town.

After two years imprisoned in this mental asylum, the young man was brought before the parole board, to review his case. After all, he was a wonderful guy, just except for the slingshot business.

The three doctors sat at this table with their white cloaks and stethoscopes around their necks looking at their patient, sincerely hoping two years in the crazy house were enough.

Their first question to him was: So, what is the first thing you are going to do when you leave this institution? His answer was: "Get my slingshot and break every window in town!"

The answer of the disappointed board of doctors was: "Looks like you want to stay here another two years!"

So, another two years go by. By now, he's been in the

slammer four years and is getting really rather bored. Don't forget, he's a brilliant, friendly, seemingly normal guy. It's just the slingshot that gets him into trouble.

So now after four years, the parole board interviews him a second time. He knows that if he mentions the slingshot again, they will keep him an additional time.

When they ask him the much feared question, "What's the first thing you are going to do when you leave here?" His answer is: "Well, to tell you the truth, there was this girl in high school I was kind of sweet on."

The doctors now look at each other very encouraged. He's not talking anymore about the slingshot. He's talking about a girl he likes. Now that's normal!

They continue to interrogate: "And then what are you going to do with her?"

He answers: "Well, I am going to invite her out to dinner, and then we will take in a movie."

The doctors are now ecstatic. Looks like this patient will be released.

The doctors ask their final question: "What will you do with your young lady friend after dinner and after the movie?"

The final answer and punchline of the joke is: "Well, after the dinner, and after the movie, I will take her home to my house and we will start 'fooling around'. I will tickle her toes, tickle the soles of her feet, tickle her up to the knees, and then when I get higher and higher up her leg and we both get really excited, then we'll take two slingshots and both of us will break every window in town."

For Islam, conquering the world is their slingshot. Annihilating all non-Moslems who refuse to convert to Islam is their slingshot. Wiping Israel off the face of the Earth is their slingshot. It is indeed a mental illness, a psychosis.

It's kind of like the US, UN, Europe, and Russia (the Quartet) forcing Israel to withdraw back to the borders of Israel pre-June 5th, 1967. First, Israel was forced by then Secretary of State Henry Kissinger in June, 1974 to withdraw from half the Golan and to return it to Syria which it did. Then Israel was forced by US President Jimmy Carter to withdraw from Sinai for peace with Egypt. Then Israel made peace with Jordan in 1994 withdrawing from lands in the Arava. Then Israel handed over land to Yasser Arafat and the PLO. Then Israel under Ariel Sharon handed over Gaza in the summer of 2005 to the Palestinians.

Of course, the slingshot is still there for Palestinian, Arab, and Moslem use against Israel. Prime Minister Ariel Sharon and his successors have broken away from the Likud party to run in the March 28th, 2006 elections so that if they win the elections, they will withdraw from virtually all of the West Bank and half of Jerusalem. All of this is for peace, peace with someone whose religion is a slingshot and for whom every window must be broken.

Iranian President Ahmedinajad recently stated, "Israel must be wiped off the face of the Earth." A few days later, the AL Aqsa Martyrs Brigades, part of the PLO, concurred: "Israel must be wiped off the face of the Earth."

On November 23rd, 2005, the Moslem Brotherhood in Egypt won a considerable chunk of the electorate in the Egyptian elections, directly threatening President Husni Mubarak's more secular rule over Egypt. What did the Moslem Brotherhood say? "Soon we will take over Egypt. We will have normal relations with all nations except for Israel. Israel must be wiped off the face of the Earth!" And this is after Israel was attacked numerous times by Egypt, and returned Sinai to Egypt under US pressure 3 times. For what? For the slingshot. For people who have a mental illness: Israel must be wiped off the face of the Earth.

If someone invites you to negotiate a multi-billion dollar contract with someone in a mental institution, you know that nothing will ever come of it. The guy in the crazy house is psychotic, living in castles in the air. In spite of all your best intentions, you cannot wrap up a deal with someone who's nuts. The world is trying to convince Israel to negotiate with an enemy that is certifiably psychotic.

So Islam is not a religion of peace. Islam is not a religion. Islam is a psychosis.

There can never be peace between Israel and Islam, or the rest of the world and Islam for that matter.

DECEPTION NUMBER 3:

Islam claims Allah is God, and God is Allah.

To understand this deception, Allah and God must be defined.

Firstly, let us define who is God. Our God, the God of the Jews and Christians is the God of Abraham, Isaac and Jacob. This God has a book known as the Bible. In it are delineated genealogies, laws and ethics.

Firstly, we read about the forefathers, Abraham, Isaac and Jacob. Ishmael and Esau were rejected by God because they were "wild donkeys (Gen. 16:12) and men of the sword (Gen. 27:40). Ishmael's hand would be against every man, and every man's hand against him; and would dwell in the face of all his brethren (fighting).

Yet Islam under Mohammed adopts Ishmael, the wild donkey, as the chosen son of Abraham. In fact Islam has a holiday called Id-al-Adha which celebrates the near sacrifice of Ishmael by Abraham in Mecca, Arabia and not the near sacrifice of Isaac by Abraham at Mt. Moriah in Jerusalem, Israel. By the way, it is interesting that Jerusalem, a city holy to Jews and Christians is never mentioned once in the Koran while Mecca, holy to the Moslems, is never once in the Bible, another irreconcilable difference between Judeo-Christianity and Islam. The two systems will be shown to be diametrically opposed to each other throughout this book.

For those who believe in God, it appears repeatedly that God's choice with Abraham is for Isaac. It's not mentioned once, but five times! Firstly, in Gen: 17:18-21, when God advises Abraham that he is about to father a second child, Isaac, Abraham responds: "Oh that Ishmael might live before Thee!" And God said: "Nay, but Sarah thy wife shall bear thee a son; and thou shall call his name Isaac; and I will establish my covenant for his seed after him. And as for Ishmael, I have heard thee; behold I have blessed him, and will make him fruitful, and will multiply him exceedingly; twelve princes shall he beget, and I will make him a great nation. But my covenant will I establish with Isaac, whom Sarah shall bear unto thee at this set time in the next year." Yet Islam claims that Ishmael was the chosen son.

The second time God refers specifically to Isaac and not to Ishmael is in Gen: 21:8-14: And the child grew (Isaac) and was weaned. And Abraham made a great feast on the day that Isaac was weaned. And Sarah saw the son of Hagar the Egyptian, whom she had borne unto Abraham (Ishmael) making sexual sport (with Isaac). Wherefore, she said unto Abraham: 'Cast out this bondwoman and her son; for the son of this bondwoman shall not be heir with my son, even with Isaac.' And the thing was very grievous in Abraham's sight on account of his son, Ishmael. And God said unto Abraham: 'Let it not be grievous in thy sight because of the lad, and because of thy bondwoman; in all that Sarah says unto thee, hearken unto her voice; for in Isaac shall seed be called to thee. And also of the son of the bondwoman will I

35

make a nation, because he is thy seed. And Abraham rose up early in the morning, and took bread and a bottle of water, and gave it unto Hagar, putting it on her shoulder, and the child, and sent her away; and she departed, and strayed in the wilderness of Beersheba." Yet Islam claims that Ishmael was the chosen son.

The third time God refers to the exclusivity of Isaac as the chosen son is in Genesis 22:1&2: "And it came to pass after these things that God did prove Abraham, and said unto him: 'Abraham'; and he said 'Here am I." And He said: "Take now thy son, THINE ONLY SON, whom thou loves, even Isaac, and get thee into the land of Moriah; and offer him there for a burnt offering upon one of the mountains which I will tell thee of.' Yet Islam celebrates Id-al-Adha, the holiday commemorating the almost-sacrifice not of Isaac but of Ishmael, and where, on Mt. Moriah? No, for Moslems, it is in Mecca at the sight of the pagan black stone: the Qa'abah. Is God confused, or is one of the two systems wrong? Either Judeo-Christianity is right or Islam is right, but not both of them.

The fourth time God shows his favoritism to Isaac is when Abraham has more children with his new wife, Ketura as well as other concubines. In chapter 25 of Genesis it says: "And Abraham took another wife, and her name was Keturah. And she bore him Zimram, and Jokshan, and Medan, and Midian, and Ishbak, and Shuah. And Jokshan begot Shbeba, and Dedan. And the sons of Dedan were Asshurim, and Letushim, and Leummim. And the sons of Midian: Ephah, and Epher, and Hanoch, and Abida, and Eldaah. All these were the children of Keturah. And Abraham gave all that he had unto Isaac. But unto the sons of the concubines, that Abraham had, Abraham gave gifts; and he sent them away from Isaac his son.

36

Finally, the fifth mention of Isaac being the chosen son, and not Ishmael is in chapter 25 verse 19: And these are the generations of Isaac, Abraham's son: Abraham begot Isaac. Period. No more Ishmael. And no more sons of the concubines. God has established his chosen genealogy.

Let's go on to the next generation. Again, we have a father, Isaac, who actually prefers the elder son, Esau, over the younger son, Jacob. Just as Abraham loved Ishmael, in spite of his wildness, maybe even more so, so did Isaac love Esau. But God chooses Isaac over Ishmael and Jacob over Esau. Perhaps the answer to this question lies in the word "sword".

When Jacob moves quickly to outmaneuver his brother, Esau, and "clinch" the blessing of the first-born, Esau then gets a strange blessing from his father: (Gen. 27:40) "You will live by the sword."

When Esau sees the bitterness his two Canaanite wives cause Isaac, Esau goes off to marry the daughter(s) of his uncle Ishmael Mahalath and Bosmat. What Jacob did with his uncle Laban by marrying his first cousins Rachel and Leah, so did Esau with his uncle Ishmael. And then, Esau went off to live with his uncle Ishmael. Esau thus became an Ishmaelite: Birds of a feather flock together.

So there is a dichotomy here. Abraham, Isaac and Jacob are shepherds and farmers. Ishmael and Esau are hunters and men of the sword. What is the difference?

Shepherds raise animals. They see the offspring of the animals. They are part of God's creation plan. Hunters and men of the sword see the deaths of animals and human beings. They are part of God's destruction plan.

Which plan will God choose? Which forefathers will he choose? Obviously, God will choose those of the creation plan over those of the destruction plan. Who does Allah choose? Allah chooses the hunters and killers.

Let's go to the New Testament. It says seven times in the New Testament that God is the God of Abraham, Isaac and Jacob. It never mentions Ishmael. Indeed, the very first Gospel, the very first chapter, the very first words of the New Testament deal in a genealogy leading to the birth of Jesus of Nazareth. Again, we read the names of Abraham, Isaac and Jacob, not Ishmael. Ishmael is nowhere to be seen.

And so for the Jew and Christian, another commonality uniting us is the genealogy of Abraham, Isaac and Jacob.

Any Jew who legitimizes Islam is de-legitimatizing the lineage holy to the Jews by legitimizing Ishmael and negating the lineage stipulated by God. Such a Jew becomes an infidel and heretic to Judaism.

And any Christian who legitimizes Islam not only violates the Old Testament holy to the Jew and Christian, but even de-legitimizes Jesus of Nazareth and his Jewish lineage. Such a Christian becomes an infidel and heretic to Christianity.

By the way, in an interesting side-note, it is known that the Moslem agenda is making strenuous efforts to disprove the existence of the Temple, first or second in Jerusalem.

Of course, it is a given in Islam that the 24 books of the Old Testament, the Tanakh, are a distortion of the truth and that neither the first nor second temples ever existed.

In a recent meeting I had with the Vatican Ambassador to Israel Archbishop Pietro Sambi, he related to me how he had met with the head of the Waqf, or the custodianship for the Aqsa and Omar mosques built on the grounds of the Temple in Jerusalem. When the head of the Waqf told Archbishop Sambi that, "Of course, it is historic fact that the 1st and 2nd Temples never existed," the archbishop then asked, "So where exactly did Jesus walk and preach." So the Islamic

38

truth is to deny the truth of the Jews and the Christians. Don't confuse Moslems with the facts. Their minds are made up. They live in the 1001 Arabian Nights.

So we Jews and Christians know who our God is: The God of Abraham, Isaac and Jacob.

Now, let us define who the god of Islam is His name is Allah Al-Ilahi. Allah was the moon god, the sword god, the war god of ancient Mecca and Medina, one of 360 pagan gods.

When Mohammed decided to create his new religion, Islam, he decided to abolish 359 other pagan gods, and crown Allah al-Ilahi as "the one and only god."

What made him do it?

Firstly, Mohammed was an illiterate camel caravan driver who married his first wife, Hadija, who was the owner of the camels. So now he became the owner of the camels and very prominent in Mecca.

As a camel caravan driver, and later owner, Mohammed came into contact with his customers who were primarily Jewish and Christian merchants seeking to trade their goods from the Byzantine Empire southward to Yemen and Africa and eastward to what is to today Oman and the Emirates on the Persian Gulf coast.

Mohammed heard the Jews and Christians preaching their monotheistic system which was superior to the out-dated pagan system of Mecca and decided, "The Jews and Christians were right. God is a monotheistic God."

Mohammed's problem was two-fold. He had an enormous ego, and secondly, he suffered from a form of epilepsy which caused him to frequently fall to the ground in uncontrollable fits of shaking, frothing at the mouth and choking. It was during these epileptic fits that Mohammed heard voices, something similar to what people close to death experience.

The word for a voice in Greek is "demon". Mohammed heard voices. Mohammed heard demons. Indeed, it says in the Koran that Mohammed listened to the "Jinns." Most uninitiated people fail to understand this term. The correct term in English would be the "genies". Mohammed listened to the genies, the mystical appearances when the Aladdin's Lamp would be rubbed.

Mohammed wasn't sure what the voices meant. Was he a prophet or a fool that he heard voices? He asked his beloved wife, Hadija, and her answer was, basically, of course you are prophet.

So now, Mohammed confronts the Jews and Christians whom he admires and with whom he is in daily contact and makes the great announcement: "I am the latest and greatest of all the prophets! I am greater than Moses (for the Jews) and greater than Jesus (for the Christians).

Considering that Mohammed never ever performed any miracles was a 40 year-old illiterate, barefoot camel driver, the Jews and Christians saw him as an amusing figure not to be taken seriously. They rejected him.

This was the classic example of rejection, of love unrequited. Now Mohammed plotted vengeance against the Jews and the Christians who were considered one people, The People of the Book, or Ahel al-Kitab.

Mohammed decided he was going to create a religion, Islam, greater than the Judeo-Christian religion. He was going to create a god greater than God. In order to do that, Mohammed adopted the Judeo-Christian concept of monotheism, but replaced the God of Abraham, Isaac and Jacob with Allah al-Illahi, the moon good, sword god and war god of ancient Mecca and Medina. He would abolish all 359 other gods and crown this 360th god as a monotheistic god, the greatest of all of them.

Besides, the God of the Jews and Christians is that sissy, wimpy God who hates the sword, a peace God. And His most important commandments are to love God and our fellow as ourselves. "We Mohammedans will teach the Jews and Christians a lesson! Our god is a macho god. Our god is the god of the sword. And he can lick the Judeo-Christian god or any god for that matter. Our god is greater than their God. Allahu Akbar."

Allahu Akbar is the call to prayer from the mosques throughout the world. It is also the battle cry of Moslems when they go to war against anyone even against themselves. The mainline media translates this as "God is great!" But that's not what it really means. Kebir in Arabic means great. Akbar is diminutive of Kebir, and it means "greater". What Moslems are really saying: "Our god is greater than their god." Or in the case of the Judeo-Christian God of Abraham, Isaac, and Jacob, "Our god, the god of Ishmael, the true heir of Abraham, the god of the sword is greater than that sissy, wimpy peace and love God of the Jews and Christians."

For Christians it is too simple. Allah is Satan. According to Christian theology, Lucifer, Satan, was a fallen angel from Heaven because he said he was greater than God. So not only is Allah not God, Allah is the opposite of God. Allah al-Ilahi is Satan himself. What the Moslems believe in is the opposite of what the Judeo-Christians believe. We are talking about polarities.

Another polarity that must be mentioned is that the God of Abraham, Isaac and Jacob loves the Jews. It says in the Bible that the Jews are the "apple of God's eye" (Zach 2:8) and that God's covenant with the Jews is eternal and everlasting. Is God a liar? But Allah hates the Jews and is a liar.

In Christian theology, the Christians believe they are grafted into the Jewish people as branches onto an olive tree. Why would the Christians believe they are grafted onto the Jewish tree if God hated the Jews? And if God grafted the Christians into the Jewish tree, does he love or hate the Christians? Obviously, he loves both the Jews and the Christians. But Allah hates the Christians as well.

Does God love or hate the Hindus and Buddhists? Both Jews and Christians agree that God loves all His children, all human beings. But Allah hates the pagans as well.

Does God love or hate the Moslems? The God of Abraham, Isaac and Jacob loves all human beings, and this includes the Moslems. They, too, are pagans, but God loves them because they are created in the image of God.

Does Allah love the Moslems? No. After the Moslems kill off all the non-Moslems, then Allah will turn the Shi'ites against the Sunnis and vice versa until there are no more Moslems left. Allah's plan, thus, is to kill all the human beings on the face of the Earth, because human beings are in God's image and Allah doesn't like it. Allah is Satan. In Jewish terminology, Satan is the "evil inclination."

Let's look at some quotes from the Koran and the Hadith:

Sura V: verse 51: Believers, take neither Jews nor Christians for your friends. They are friends with one another. Whoever of you seeks their friendship shall become one of their number. Allah does not guide the wrongdoer. (Meaning: a death sentence). Nope, doesn't look like Allah likes the Jews or Christians.

Sura V: verse 57: Believers, do not seek the friendship of the infidels and those who were given the Book before you, who have made of your religion a jest and a pastime. Have fear of Allah, if you are true believers.

Sura V: verse 60: Say: 'Shall I tell you who will receive a worse reward from Allah? Those whom Allah has cursed (the Jews and Christians) and with whom He has been angry, transforming them into apes and swine, and those who serve the devil. Worse (death) is the plight of these, and they have strayed further from the path.'

My wife, Rachel, an Arabic language media monitor for Israel Radio picked up a speech in the summer of 2002 by Sheikh Akram a-Sabri, mufti of Jerusalem. In a Friday afternoon preaching at the mosque on the Temple Mount, Sheik Sabri said: "Kill the Jews. Kill the Christians. Kill the Israelis. Kill the Americans. Kill the monkeys and kill the pigs (apes and swine). This speech, of course, gets its inspiration from the above verse 60 of Sura V of the Koran.

In the summer of 2003, I used this quote during speeches I made in seven cities in Switzerland. I made first page of Al-Watan, Saudi Arabia's biggest newspaper and soon after in the biggest circulation Arabic daily in the world: Al Sharq al Awsat. They claimed I was a senior intelligence officer. (I wish I was). They claim I was sent by Jerusalem to mobilize the Christians world over. (I wish I was.) And then they said that I launched the worst attack against Islam. To that I say: Amen!

From the Hadith (a collection of sayings and traditions attributed to Mohammed, but not included in the Koran), there is a teaching that on the Day of Judgment, there will be a final battle and Moslems will annihilate ever last living Jew in the whole world.

Now, some Jews will temporarily evade their deaths by hiding behind rocks and trees. On that day, Allah will give mouths to the rocks and trees, and they will call out: "Oh Muslim pursuers, there is a Jew hiding behind come and kill him."

Again, my wife comes into the picture. Rachel is a beautiful woman and for twelve years was an Arabic

43

language program announcer on Israel TV. Even though she retired years ago from this position, many Arabic speaking people still treat her like a TV superstar.

In fact, there is a gas station in French Hill where we regularly fill up with gas, change our oil and wash the car. The attendants there are young Arab Moslems from the village of Isawiya adjacent to the French Hill neighborhood. These young men just adore Rachel, even if she is no longer on the TV screen. They always give her "red carpet treatment".

Not long ago, however, one of them said to my wife: "Rachel, you know we love you. We always take good care of you. But you know we have a problem with you because you are Jew. And you know that Allah will soon give mouths to the rocks and trees. And they will call out to us saying, 'There is a Jew hiding behind me. Come and kill him (or her).' And you know we love you. We don't want to kill you, but we will if you don't become a Moslem! So please become a Moslem!"

What is the conclusion? If the God of Abraham, Isaac and Jacob loves the Jews and loves all humans, and Allah hates the Jews and all humans, clearly God and Allah are not the same. They are opposites. They are polarities. Allah = Satan.

DECEPTION NUMBER 4:

Moslems will try to deceive Christians by saying that the Jesus of Islam is the same as the Jesus of Christianity. The only problem with that is that Jesus of Islam is coming back a second time as an Arabic speaking Moslem. He will appear on the Golan Heights, then descend to the coastal plain near Lod (where Israel's international airport is located), meet the anti-Christ in battle and slay him with a spear.

Then Jesus the Moslem will go up to Jerusalem, pray

with 400,000 Moslems during the morning prayers on the Temple Mount. Then Jesus the Moslem will come down with 400,000 Moslem followers, break every cross and destroy every church. Then he will destroy all the synagogues.

On this Day of Judgment, all Jews and Christians, the People of the Book, who have not embraced Allah as God, Mohammed as the greatest of the prophets, and who have not converted to Islam will have their throats slit by Jesus Christ the Moslem.

I don't think so.

By the way, one of the greatest accomplishments, in my opinion, of Mel Gibson's movie the "Passion of Christ" was to show that Jesus spoke Aramaic and Hebrew, but not Arabic. This runs contrary to Islamic teachings.

DECEPTION NUMBER 5:

The Koran is the divine, infallible word of Allah to Mohammed. In my first book, "Is Fanatic Islam a Global Threat?" I reveal private investigation work that I conducted in Tucson, Arizona, researching the assassination of Rashad Khalifa, the imam of the mosque there on January 30th 1990.

He was killed by two Black Muslim hit teams sent to Tucson, from Colorado Springs, Colorado and Williamsport, Pennsylvania on orders from Pakistan because he had proven mathematically that the Koran had satanic verses in it.

He did this mathematically by proving that the numerology of 19 appeared repeatedly throughout the Koran. The number 19 has numerous Jewish connotations, and indeed there are Jewish traditions that the Koran was written by a Jewish rabbi kidnapped by the illiterate nomadic warriors who conquered the world for Allah, but who knew not how to write.

There are also Christian traditions from certain Eastern

45

Orthodox churches which claim that the Koran was written by a priest from one of these denominations.

The Koran has Bible, Agadah, Midrash and Talmud in it. These are all Jewish literary genre that only rabbis could know.

I believe the Koran was written by both a Jewish rabbi and a Christian priest under duress to create a book that nomads could never write. The Koran had to be written in such a way as to surpass the Bible of the Jew and the Christian.

However, the Koran is a book of gibberish, of evil verses abrogating holy verses.

While it includes meritorious verses taken from the Bible, these verses are then negated by other verses, satanic verses, murderous verses which are the ones Moslems follow.

Again, the two most important commandments for Jews and Christians are Love the Lord thy God and Love thy neighbor as thyself. These two verses are non-existent in the Koran or Hadith.

I also have not found the 10 Commandments in the Koran, except maybe for Commandment number 6: Thou shall not kill. But the only problem with the Koran's version is as follows: Sura 17: verse 33.

"Though shall not kill any man whom Allah has forbidden you to kill, except for a just cause."

The Koran is a replacement theology book. Islam's plan was to show that it was greater then the Judeo-Christian ethic, that Allah was greater than God and that the Koran was greater than the Bible.

By the way, even though the rabbi and priest were promised their freedom upon completion of the Koran, they were then stoned to death after completing the work they were kidnapped for. The Moslems killed and inherited.

But I think it is fair to say for any scholar of the Bible,

Agadah, Midrash and Talmud that the Koran doesn't even rise to the level of plagiarism, because the Koran is a mean, evil distorted book of abrogations.

Islam is not a religion of love.

Islam is not a religion of peace. (Islam is not a religion but a psychosis).

Allah is not God but Satan.

Mohammad was a sick (epileptic) and evil murderer, rapist, thief, and liar.

Jesus of Islam is not the Jesus of Christianity but the murderer of all Jews and Christians.

And finally, the Koran is not the divine infallible word of Allah to Mohammed, but a collection of some biblical, midrashic and Talmudic verses all contaminated by the murderous character of the Islamic psychosis which adopted the wild ass Ishmael as its forefather. Islam's inheritance to the world is to live in the face of humanity and to die in the face of humanity.

CHAPTER THREE

Islamic Invasions, Past, Present and Future

In order to understand 1,400 years of Islamic conquest and expansion, it is necessary to return to the life of Mohammed and the inspiration behind the new ideology he created.

Again, it is easy today in the 21st century to look around ourselves, and enjoy 100% hindsight and wisdom as to the disasters that Islam has brought to the world. But the patterns of destruction we see Islam bringing to the world today are the same as they were during the life and after the death of Mohammed.

For example, on September 11th, 2001, Islamic suicide warriors brought death and destruction to the United States bringing down the Twin Towers of the World Trade Center in New York City, blowing up part of the Pentagon in Washington, DC, as well as in the crash in Pennsylvania of an airliner which never made it to its intended target, the Capitol in Washington, DC. More than 3,000 Americans and others died in these attacks.

Some people saw the attack on September 11th as an attack on the US. In my opinion, it was more than that. This was an attack on the economic nerve center of the world on Wall Street in Manhattan. The idea was to bring down the American economy, thereby destroying the economy of the West, thereby destroying the economy of the world. This was an attack against all of humanity.

How do we see this in the life and death of Mohammed? As mentioned previously, Mohammed was a camel caravan driver, and later owner. He knew all the routes of the camel caravans, and when and how to attack. When his customers, the Jews and Christians, refused to recognize Mohammed as the latest and the greatest of all the prophets, he knew when and where to strike at the Jews and Christians: in their pockets.

In order to mobilize the pagan Arabian tribes to convert to his new religion, Mohammed promised them plunder and spoils. This was payment for their joining his armies and basically leaving scorched earth everywhere they went.

Within a short time, all commerce with Jews and Christians in Arabia came to a halt. Jewish and Christian colonies with farms and orchards were also destroyed as were entire populations of Jews and Christians in the Arabian Peninsula. Mohammed completely destroyed the economy of Arabia at that time.

Even Judeo-Christian groups which surrendered were then massacred by Mohammed with the women and children taken over as slaves and converted to Islam. Mohammed's northernmost conquest was what is today Aqaba in the most southwestern part of Jordan. Now, after the death of Mohammed, is followers had to look further away for new conquests that they could plunder and destroy because Mohammed left Arabia as scorched Earth.

After the death of Mohammed, there was a schism between a group of leaders led by Abu Bakr and the immediate family of Mohammed. The former slaughtered the latter group and this became the never ending war up until today between the Sunnis and the Shi'ites. It makes the Christian Wars of Reformation look like a Sunday school picnic. The seeds of this internecine self-destruction were planted 1,400 years ago in which Moslems slaughter Moslems.

Again, this is prophesied in Genesis 16:12: "He (Ishmael) shall be a wild ass of a man: his hand shall be against every man, and every man's hand against him; and he shall dwell in the face of all his brethren."

In Genesis 25:28: "And they (the Ishmaelites) dwelt from Havilah unto Shur, that is before Egypt, as thou goest toward Asshur: and he (Ishmael) died in the face of his brethren." He who lives by the sword dies by the sword.

But let us return to the slaughter of the non-Moslems first. As commerce in Arabia was systematically destroyed by Mohammed, since all Judeo-Christian commerce was plundered, new areas had to now be conquered to continue to provide payment to these desert tribes that knew nothing else but fighting.

This led to Islamic invasions north, south, east and west. Mohammed died in 632 AD (CE). Six years later (638) Omar al-Khattab conquers the Holy Land. Here we find three groups of interest: Byzantine Christians, Jews and Zoroastrian Persians.

It was in the year 614 that the Zoroastrian (pagan) armies of Persia conquered the Holy Land thus liberating the Jews who until then lived under extreme persecution from the Byzantine Empire.

With liberation by the Persians, the Jews now began to reconsider building a Third Temple on Mt Moriah. The Second Temple, it must be remembered had been destroyed by the Romans in the year 70. Historically, relations between the Jews and the Persians had always been good. The Persian Emperor Cyrus is described in the Bible as "messiah" for helping return the Jews to the Holy Land after decades of exile at the hands of the Babylonians in 586 BCE. It was Cyrus who helped the Jews build the Second Temple.

The famous holiday of Purim, and the Scroll of Esther speak of the Jewish victory over the evil Haman who was the prime minister of the Persian King Artaxerxes. But Haman, who was defeated, was actually descended from Agag and Amalek, ancient enemies of Israel. Once Haman was defeated, there were no problems with the Persian people.

So basically, we see an alliance between the Persians and the Jews, against the Christian Byzantines. Omar al-Khattab, the Arab conqueror thus aligned himself with the Christians in order to defeat the Jews and Persians. One must not forget that the Persians were considered pagans to be immediately put to the sword, whereas the Jews were slaughtered by the Moslems throughout Arabia and in Yemen. This was to continue in the Holy Land.

Also Omar al-Khattab had an agreement with the Christian Archbishop Sophronios: No Jews in Jerusalem. This became known as the Sophronios Agreement between the Byzantine Church and the conquering Moslems.

The Arab armies continued to sweep northward into Lebanon, and eastward into Iraq and Iran. Then Islam moved westward conquering Egypt. Now the Coptic Christians, the original descendants of the Pharaohs, were subdued and eventually were made into a minority in Egypt. Within about 80 years of the death of Mohammed, the Arabian armies reached Morocco and the Atlantic Ocean.

Since within a very short time, the Arab invaders found themselves to be in the minority in all the countries they conquered, agreements were drawn up with the Christian and Jewish communities that these communities were not forced to convert to Islam (for now). It was only the pagans who had to choose between conversion to Islam or the sword. Most pagans converted to Islam.

The Islamic ideology was that Jews and Christians, the People of the Book, were to be "left alone" as long as they swore allegiance to these new Arab-Islamic conquerors and promised to become subservient to their Islamic overlords. The Jews and Christians thus became known as "dhimmis".

Indeed, the Moslem invaders were the greatest conquerors of their time, but that did not change the fact that they were illiterate. They needed the Jews and Christians to become part of their empire by helping run the empire. Jews and Christians were knowledgeable in reading, writing and arithmetic, and so they were tolerated as long as they served their Moslem overlords.

Jews and Christians had to wear clothing demarcating them clearly as not being Moslems. Jews and Christians had to walk in the street and not on side walks. They could not ride donkeys if a Moslem was walking. They could not be higher than a Moslem. The minarets of the mosques had to be higher than the churches and synagogues. And finally, Jews and Christians had to pay the "Jiziya" or poll-tax.

At first the Jiziya was not exorbitant, but later it became too onerous for Jews and Christians to pay. So the solution became converting to Islam to avoid payment. This was one of the ways that over the centuries Islam "digested" the various communities that had originally settled the countries they conquered.

Finally, as the Moslems became the majority in each country, as they learned to read and write, as Jewish and Christian scholars converted to Islam to avoid paying the onerous Jiziyah, it became easier for Islamic leaders to become radical and then forcefully convert, kill or exile the Jews and the Christians who had not as of yet converted.

It was also during this time, I believe, that the Koran was written. According to an Iranian rabbi living in Jerusalem, the Koran was written about 80 years after the death of Mohammed. It was based on teachings handed down orally, as well as some teachings written on leaves and parchments. But it was up to the rabbi, some call him Ovadya ben Shalom or Shalom ben Ovadya, to put all this material together co-opting teachings from the Bible, Midrash and Talmud.

If this was indeed 80 years after the death of Mohammed, then it was contemporary with the Islamic invasion of Spain in 711. It must be remembered that Mohammed's plan was to create a religion greater than the Judeo-Christian religion. He had to create a god greater than the God of Abraham, Isaac, and Jacob.

But how could all this be, surmised Mohammad's heirs, if Islam did not have a book greater than the Bible? So, again, as I stated before, it must have been at about this time that a rabbi and probably a priest, as well, from the Armenian, Coptic, or Assyrian Orthodox churches were "pressed into service" to complete the Koran and then stoned to death by the illiterate Mohammedans instead of being released as originally promised.

With the Islamic invasion of Spain, Portugal and France in 711, we find a remarkable trend in history. Western Europe, which had just adopted Christianity four centuries before, was about to be overwhelmed by the Islamic invaders.

We mustn't forget that with the collapse of the Western Roman Empire, it was the Eastern Roman Empire, Byzantium, which basically took over as the bastion of Christianity. Western Europe was overrun by pagan hordes of invaders, Goths, Visigoths, Huns, Lombards, Magyars, and others. Christianity's hold on Western Europe and was tenuous at best.

54

The Islamic armies swept all the way to what is today the Belgian border. They conquered Spain, Portugal and France in 21 years. They seemed unstoppable. All that remained of Christian Western Europe was England, Germany, the Rhine valley and northern Italy. Scandinavia of the Vikings and Russia were still pagan. Russian Orthodox Christianity was only adopted in 995 AD (CE) after being brought to the pagan Russian tribes by Cyril and Methodius.

We also must remember that the Moslems conquered southern Italy all the way up to Rome. In 868, the Moslems threatened to sack Rome if the Pope did not come up with the extortion money the Moslems demanded. The Islamic conquest of southern Italy lasted 600 years and left its mark in the culture and the language spoken in southern Italy and Sicily. By the way, the language spoken on the Catholic Island of Malta is Arabic, very similar to that spoken in Alexandria, Egypt. The language of Sicily is somewhere between Maltese and Italian, but the Arabic influence is there in Sicily together with that of the Greeks and Phoenicians as well.

Western Europe seemed doomed to Islamic conquest. It was only at the battle of Poitiers, France in 732 that Charles Martell and his commander Roland turned the tide of battle and began what the Spanish call the "Reconquista" or re-conquest of Western Europe, something that was to take 760 years, until 1492.

Again, it must be emphasized that there was not only one Islamic invasion across the Straits of Gibraltar, but many. Moroccan armies were constantly crossing over into Spain to reinforce Islamic rule in Spain, Portugal and France, but just as the tide comes in and then recedes in spite of numerous waves hitting the shore, so, too, did Islam get eventually pushed further back southward, out of France, out of Portugal by 1147, and finally out of the Moorish Kingdom of Granada in the south of Spain by 1492. This was a victory for Christendom after 760 years of warfare.

But at the same time the wars of re-conquest were taking place in the Iberian Peninsula, the popes in Rome called for five crusades to liberate the Holy Land from Islamic rule. The period known today as the "Crusades" began in 1096 and ended with the defeat of King Richard the Lionhearted of England in 1293 after the disastrous defeat of the Christians in the Battle of the Horns of Hittin near Tiberias. This was indeed a world war between Christianity and Islam, and it had many fronts. In the case of the Holy Land, unlike the Iberian Peninsula, the Christians were finally defeated. Salah-ed-Din or Saladin as he is known in English was the Kurdish leader of the Islamic forces who defeated the Christians, and thus, today, Saladin has become the role model for all Islamic children in today's wars of religion between Islam and the rest of the World.

Even during the Gulf War in 1991, when Saddam Hussein launched 39 Scud missiles at targets in Israel, Palestinian Moslems cheered as the missiles flew overhead from East to West, shouting: "Oh, Saddam, dear Saddam, hit Tel-Aviv. Oh Saddam, dear Saddam hit the cross!" This was because Palestinian Moslems view the Jews of Israel today as merely, the modern day Crusaders sent to the Middle East by America and the West. And the Moslems believed that Saddam Hussein was their role model, a modern-day Saladin.

It is often very hard, if not impossible, for people in the US, Canada and other former colonies of Europe in the Americas, to fully appreciate wars of religion that took place in Spain for 760 years or Crusades of 200 years, or wars with the Turks in Eastern Europe for a thousand years, when the America's history starts with the Pilgrims landing on Plymouth Rock in 1621 and has lasted for less than four centuries.

Even the history of Latin America only started with Christopher Columbus in 1492. But still, this is just over five centuries of history compared to 760 years of wars of re-conquest in Western Europe. And even in the Mexican city of Matamoros, just across the border from Brownsville, Texas, most young Mexicans have no clue where the name Matamoros came from. (Matamoros means Moor Killer).

What North American, South American, and Australasian history have in common is virtually no contact or experience with Islamic invasions until now basically. And if young people are not history buffs, they cannot understand the phenomenon of September 11, 2001. But this attack was nothing new. It was merely an extension of wars that started with the death of Mohammed in 632 AD and have never stopped. These are wars designed first and foremost to destroy the economy of the enemies of Allah.

What about Eastern Europe? After the wars of Western Europe (Iberia) and after the Crusades in the Holy Land, came the Ottoman Turkish invasions of Europe from the East.

There seems to be a "disconnect" when history is being taught in schools. I will never forget when I went to school in New York in my youth Christopher Columbus was described to us as a man who crossed the Atlantic to prove the World was round. We were told that he was also looking for new trade routes to the East for spices and products the Europeans had gotten used to. Another typically American insight was that Christopher Columbus was offering his services to Spain to get an edge over other European powers. All of this is great for a Steven Spielberg movie, but ignores the real reasons for Columbus's odyssey across the Atlantic, and the fact that Christopher Columbus saved Europe from being vanquished by Islam through his discovery of the new continents.

This is only partially right. To understand Christopher Columbus, to understand Ferdinand and Isabella of Spain in 1492, one needs to know the history of the Ottoman Turkish conquest of the Byzantine Empire and Eastern Europe. What happened in Eastern Europe affected Western Europe.

Although Constantinople fell to the Islamic Turks as late as 1453, Serbia was conquered in 1389 at the Battle of Kosovo Field. The Turks had already conquered Greece, Bulgaria, Romania, Albania, and were on their way to conquering Hungary, Ukraine, Russia and Poland. The Turks were at the gates of Vienna for 200 years! Most Austrian students have this fact indelibly engraved in their collective memories.

What does this have to do with Christopher Columbus in Spain? The Turkish conquest of Constantinople, now renamed Istanbul, effectively cut off the trade routes from Christian Europe to China and India. The Italian city-states such as Venice and Genoa which had established trade bases and forts in Cyprus, and Constantinople along the "Silk Road" were now all out of business because of the Turks. Europe was now being slowly starved and strangled by the Moslem Turks.

Whereas the Spanish, Portuguese and French faced Moorish/Arab invaders, now it was the turn of Italy, Austria, and Germany to defend Western Europe from Ottoman Islamic invaders from the East. It must also be remembered that in 1204 the Western (Catholic) Christians arrived in the Byzantine Empire and massacred Eastern Greek Christians, thus weakening the Byzantine Empire and helping to hasten its demise.

It must also be remember that the Crusades massacred

58

the Jews wherever they could be found. This is also one of the reasons that led to the Jewish people preferring alliances with Moslem leaders who were less harsh to the Jews during this period.

But getting back to Christopher Columbus, he was now an unemployed Genoese sailor offering his services first to Portugal which replied negatively because the Portuguese believed that the best or only route to the Far East was by going around the Cape of Good Hope at the southern tip of Africa (the route of Vasco da Gama) and then to Spain's Queen Isabella who had to sell off her jewelry in order to pay for the Nina, Pinta and Santa Maria, the three ships of Christopher Columbus's first fleet. This shows you how miserably poor Spain was before Columbus departed on his historic voyage into the unknown.

Christopher Columbus' discover brought much needed wealth to Spain, not from the East Indies, as originally planned, but from the new territories Columbus discovered. Not only were gold and silver flowing into Spanish coffers, but so, too, were chocolate, coffee, potatoes and tomatoes as well as tobacco.

More importantly, North and South America and later Australasia became Christian settlement areas. Christendom was no longer just a few besieged countries in Western or Eastern Europe. Christopher Columbus tipped the scales decisively in favor of Christianity, another nail in Islam's coffin at that time.

In order to understand Queen Isabella, I wanted to share something from my military experiences in the Israeli Defense Forces. My wife, Rachel, and I recently visited Spain. We flew from Belgium to the little county airport in Valladolid in the north of Spain. There we rented a car and drove south three hours to Madrid, the capital of Spain.

Spain is mountainous country but the road we drove on really reminded me of Israel and in some ways of New Mexico. Spain is a mesa a country mostly elevated on a high plateau. But once you are on top of the plateau, it is mostly a level drive.

From Madrid, Rachel and I drove to Toledo, the famous Jewish city of antiquity, also a relatively flat drive and from there, we continued southward on Highway 5 toward the crossroads junction of Bailen also flat country. Looming toward the south were the mountains of Granada.

Now, all of a sudden, it was no longer a relatively flat drive but an arduous crossing of the mountains of Andalucia. All of a sudden, "the lights went on." I now understood why Ferdinand and Isabella expelled the Jews and Moslems from Spain in 1492.

For almost all Jews, the Expulsion of 1492 from Spain is about as traumatic as the Nazi Holocaust in the 20th century. Earlier in this book, I related how I grew up in a home that had a love for Spain (because my parents were raised in Argentina), just as Spain is the mother country for all Spanish speaking people in the world. But as a Jew, there we had this love-hate relationship with Spain because of the expulsion and the torturous inquisition.

All Jews know that the Moslem invaders from Morocco were radical at first, but after they lived a few years in Iberia and came into daily live contact with the Jews and Christians, they moderated in their behavior. And indeed there were "reinforcement" invasions from Morocco when the latter invaders thought that the former Moslem invaders were "becoming too soft," on the Jews and Christians.

Indeed, by 1492, the last Moorish king of Granada, Boabdil had created this image for himself of academic, liberal and pacifist. The Golden Age of the Jews in Spain was rubbing off on the Moslems as well. The south of Spain had become a plush paradise for the Jews and Moslems as well as those Christians living amongst them. But the Christian kingdom to the North could not tolerate an Islamic foothold in the South. A showdown was inevitable.

When Ferdinand and Isabella delivered Boabdil with the ultimatum, leave Spain immediately and forfeit your kingdom or the Christian north will wage war against the Moslem/ Jewish south, Boabdil decided to forfeit his kingdom in order to spare his people the bloodshed. He believed in "no more war, no more bloodshed." War for Boabdil was barbaric and unjustifiable. He was a liberal, a pacifist. He did not believe that any war was worth it. So Boabdil abdicated his thrown. As he stood on his balcony in the beautiful palace of Granada for the last time crying at the loss of his kingdom, his mother is reputed to have said to him, "You cry like a woman for a kingdom you could not defend like a man."

It is interesting that my mother, rest in peace, told me this story. This was the history and folklore of Spain. So, aside from Spanish folklore, and getting back to military doctrine, why did the lights go on for me during this trip to Spain? All my life, I had hated and vilified Ferdinand and Isabella. All Jews do. Even my wife, Rachel, can trace her lineage back to the Expulsion from Spain in 1492.

But after our recent trip to Spain, I think, until the people read this book, that I am the only Jew in the world today who understands and respects the decisions, as horrible and cruel as they were, of Ferdinand and Isabella to expel all the Jews and Moslems from Spain. Ferdinand and Isabella had no choice. The Moslems could not be allowed to have a foothold in Spain, because that would entice other Moslems to invade. And if the Jews were allied with the Moslems, they had to leave too.

In November 1993, I had the honor of participating in an Israel Defense Forces spokesman's course. One of our briefings was about anti-aircraft missiles. Our commanders taught us just how simple it was for the Palestinians to shoot down any military or civilian aircraft trying to take off or land in Israel if the Palestinians were to control hills of Judea and Samaria. We were taught: "Whoever controls the high ground controls the plains."

That is the reason, our commanders told us, that from a military perspective, there must never be a Palestinian state. Israel on the coast will be dominated and destroyed by the Palestinians (or any adversary for that matter) who control the high grounds. That's why the lights went on.

Here we were in Spain, and we could feel the centuries of warfare between the Moslems and the Christians. Wave after wave after wave of Islamic invaders came across the Straits of Gibraltar into southern Spain making it all the way past Portugal to France, and it took 760 years for the Christians to put an end to this once and for all.

Haplessly for the Jews, they were on the side of the losers, the Moslems. It is true the Christians were considered by the Moslem/Jewish southerners in Spain as barbarians. It is true that the Moslem/Jewish culture of Granada was superior to that of the Christian north. But when it came to force of arms, the "barbarian" Christians defeated the pacifist Boabdil and that was the end of it. And if the Jews chose the losing side, they lost as well. That explains the expulsion. We were on the wrong side of history.

So, militarily and strategically speaking, what did Ferdinand and Isabella see that we in our ignorance of the 21st century do not see? The answer is very simple: the Turks. So you may ask, "But Turkey is in the eastern end of the Mediterranean. What does this have to do with Spain?"

By 1492, the Turks had extended their control all the way to the gates of Vienna. Their raiders reached the gates of Warsaw, Moscow and Kiev. Southwards, the Turks controlled Mecca and Medina and Baghdad to the East.

But most important of all, the Turks had established their sovereignty over most of North Africa including Algeria and the northern parts of Morocco, just across the Straits of Gibraltar! So the Turks, together with a possible coalition of Moroccans, Arabs and Jews who by now had lost their homes in Spain were all ready for a new Islamic invasion of the Iberian Peninsula.

Ferdinand and Isabella knew, in my opinion, that if the Moslems had any kind of a foothold whatsoever in Spain, especially in the mountains of the South, a new Islamic "invasion of reinforcements" sponsored this time by the Turks could spell disaster. This time, it might even be the end of Christianity in Spain, Portugal and even France.

In this manner, the Turks could create a pincer movement linking up the Turks to the east of Vienna with those barreling up into central Europe from Spain. The Moslems came up through the Iberian Peninsula once before, and they could do it again. How did the Spanish, after all, put an end to Turkish plans of conquest?

As person who was born and raised in the United States of America, I cannot deny that much of my thinking was shaped by what I was taught in American schools. It is also a fact that lessons learned in the Spanish speaking world of Latin America reflect Spain as the mother country, while the English speaking world including the US, Canada, Australia, etc. focuses on England as the mother country.

When I speak in churches and synagogues in the US, I always ask the following question: "Who here heard about the defeat of the Spanish Armada in 1588?" Almost invariably, all hands go up. This is because the defeat of the Spanish Armada was a great victory for the British navy and of course, for the Protestants over the Catholics.

But when I ask a similar question: "Who here heard about the Sea Battle of Lepanto of 1563 almost no one except history buffs has heard about this. "Why?" one asks. This is because this battle represents the victory of Catholic Spain over the Islamic Turkish Empire. This battle seems to have nothing to do with White Anglo-Saxon Protestant Western Europe and the United States.

But the Battle of Lepanto signaled the beginning of the end for the Turks in the Mediterranean, and the final and unconditional victory of Christianity in Spain. It wouldn't be until March 11th, 2004 that the Moslems would attack Spain again.

When I studied in American schools in the 50's and 60's, it seemed that the defeat of the Spanish Armada in 1588 was the end of Spain until the 1898 Spanish-American War put a final seal on the fate of Spain as a world power.

But the fact was that with the destruction of the Spanish Armada in 1588 by a coalition of British and Dutch navies, the Spanish could rebuild a new fleet with all the gold and silver pouring in from the Indian-slave operated mines in Peru and Mexico. But after 1588 the English navy was now the first power on the seas. The Battle of Lepanto in 1563 was the end of Turkish maritime might. The battle of the Spanish Armada in 1588 was the beginning of the end of Spanish naval might, and its replacement by the British. From then on it was: "Britannia rules the waves!" But the Spanish saved the Christian world from the Turkish navy's attacks in the Mediterranean.

Another interesting point in history was that Spain was now part of the Hapsburg Empire through marriage, so the presence of the Turks at the gates of Vienna was the same as a Turkish invasion of Spain.

It was in 1648 that the Turks began retreating from the Gates of Vienna. It was the beginning of the end of the Turkish Ottoman Empire. First it was the Magyars or Hungarians who would free themselves from the Turks after 150 years of tutelage. After this it was the turn of the Romanians, the Serbs and the Greeks. Greece received its independence in 1821. The last battles in Europe waged against the Turks were the Balkan Wars of 1902, 1903 and 1912 establishing the final borders of Bulgaria, Serbia, Greece and Macedonia. The Turks were now with their backs to the wall at the Bosporus.

Again, just as the Moslems were evicted from Christian Europe in the West in 760 years, so, too, were the Moslem Turks evicted militarily over a period of many centuries. So Christianity, it seems, emerges victorious over the Moslems in two epic struggles in Western and Eastern Europe.

Europe even succeeds for a few centuries in colonizing Moslem countries.

All seems well and fine for the Christians in the early 20th century. But the latter part of the 20th century signals a reversal of fortunes -- the third Islamic invasion of Europe. Islam is relentless in its plans to conquer Europe and the world. I call this the third and final rise of Islam before the third and final defeat.

I will expound on today's Islamic conquest of the world in Chapter V.

CHAPTER FOUR

The Development of Judeo-Christian Western Civilization and Democracy

To understand the development of Judeo-Christian Western Civilization and Democracy, I believe we must go back to Greece and Rome to glance briefly at their systems.

Greek democracy was known primarily for its two leading antagonists: Athens and Sparta.

The democracy of Athens was as follows: Women could not vote. So 50% of the population was disenfranchised. Foreigners or naturalized citizens could not vote. The only people who could vote were the landed established Athenian born citizens. So we are talking about 15% of the population. It was not really democracy yet as we know it today. More like Kuwait.

The democracy of Sparta was more like a socialist totalitarian state, where men and women were equal. Women even fought in the battles alongside men. But beware: people in Sparta did not bathe like the Athenians did. They led a very simple, austere, some people say almost Communist way of life. They were all poor, but all were equal in their poverty.

Rome for its part was some of the time Republic, some of the time Empire led by Caesars. Citizenship was to be acquired by foreigners, and slaves could be free and acquire citizenship under certain circumstances. Examples of this are Flavius Josephus who led the northern army of Judea, surrendered to Rome, and was later granted citizenship, and of course, the Apostle Paul who was a Roman when in Rome and a Jew when in Jerusalem.

But none of these systems were democratic as we know democracy today. The development of Judeo-Christian Western Civilization and Democracy had roots, of course, in the values of the Bible, but Democracy is never mentioned in the Bible. Democracy did not exist until recently.

It was the synthesis of Judaism, Christianity with Greco-Roman systems which over a period of two thousand years, and mostly in the last three centuries Judeo-Christian Western Civilization and Democracy blossomed.

With the fall of the pagan Roman Empires, East and West, we saw the establishment and entrenchment of the Church, Catholic in Rome and Byzantine Orthodox in Constantinople. Kings were usually appointed or sanctioned by the church fathers.

Church control was absolute. And kings ruled absolutely. It wasn't until the Magna Charta, that the first great charter of the personal and political liberties of the people of England, were demanded and obtained from King John in 1215.

It was the English system which pioneered in this direction. There was set in motion a system of checks and balances in which the King was no longer an absolute ruler but was accountable to the nobles and centuries later to the citizenry in general.

But these were cruel times. And like I said earlier, there were some crucial wars being waged by the Moslems and Christians in Western Europe, Eastern Europe and the Holy Land. It was the time of the Crusades. Jews and sometimes even fellow Christians who happened to belong to the wrong Christian denominations, especially Byzantine, were massacred by fellow Christians from the West.

Jews, who were hated because of Church teachings that the Jews killed Christ, were persecuted in almost every Christian land. They were expelled from York, England in 1140 (only to be brought back by the Protestant Oliver Cromwell in 1655.) It was in 1391 that the Jews were expelled by the Christians from northern Spain, or they had the option of conversion to Christianity. Many Jews left northern Spain for southern Spain only to be expelled in 1492 from southern Spain as well. Many of these Jews then fled to Islamic lands, primarily Morocco and the Turkish Empire which received these Jews as welcomed guests.

But there were many Jews who faked conversion to Catholicism in order to remain in their homes and continue enjoying the lives they had always known. Outwardly, they were now Christians, but secretly they continued to practice Judaism. These people were called Marranos, or pigs, by the Christians. The more politically correct Jewish term is conversos or converted and in Hebrew "anousim" which means forced into conversion.

As I mentioned in Chapter III, the political and religious leadership in Spain and Portugal wanted to ensure the political and religious homogeneity of the kingdoms. Jews were seen as potential allies with the Moslems, and as I said previously, 760 years of wars with the Moslems had sufficed for the Christians. They did not want a "fifth column." That's how the Jews were viewed.

There is even the experience of the some Jews who left Spain in 1492 and traveled next door to Portugal. The Catholic king there received the Jews well, but when his son wanted to marry the daughter of Ferdinand and Isabella, they demanded that the all these Jews in Portugal (who had just left Spain) be immediately converted to Catholicism as a condition for the marriage of the son and daughter.

So in 1493, all the Jews were gathered in the main square in Lisbon and priests took buckets of water from the public fountains and "baptized" tens of thousands of Jews against their will.

So now, there are all these tens of thousands of Jews who are new Christians and are highly suspect since their conversion seems not to be sincere. The Catholic authorities established the "Inquisition" to follow up on these conversions. Anyone caught practicing his or her Judaism would be tortured and burned at the stake at the infamous auto-da-fe.

Officially, the purpose of the Inquisition was to prevent heresy, but it was applied from the beginning especially with the Jewish conversos in mind. Enter King Henry VIII of England (1491-1597). He was a good Catholic who married a Princess from Spain. But when he god tired of her and fell in love with Anne Bolen, he aroused the ire of the Church when he annulled the previous marriage. Since divorce is not allowed in Catholicism, Henry VIII broke away from Rome and established his own church, the Anglican or English Church.

It was basically at this same time that Martin Luther (1483-1546) a German reformer led a Protestant Reformation against the Catholic hierarchy, and thus we see the erosion of power of the Catholic Church in Rome and the rise mostly in northern and Western Europe of different Protestant Churches.

Centuries of bloody wars of reformation ensued, some of the embers of which occasionally reignite in Northern Ireland.

70

Also, with the appearance of the Gutenberg printing press the Bible now became relatively inexpensive to acquire and accessible to all. Individuals could now study God's word without intercessors from the Church or priests giving them an interpretation which was not literal, but subservient to the Church's agenda.

And no sooner did these local churches break away from the Catholic Church in Rome, that they imposed their own totalitarian form of doctrine which caused many Bible reading and believing Christians to also rebel against these new mainline Protestant churches.

Now that the Americas were discovered, and the various European colonies became open to settlers from the Old Europe, people seeking religious freedom from the intolerance of both the Catholic and state churches now voted with their feet and emigrated to the new territories. It was indeed groups like the Puritans, Pilgrims, Quakers, Huguenots, Amish and Mennonites who fled the persecution in Europe for the freedom of the new colonies in the Americas.

The following is an article from © 2005 WorldNetDaily. com.

How did America go from Pilgrims seeking freedom to express their Judeo-Christian beliefs to today's discrimination against those very beliefs in the name of tolerance?

The journey of the evolution of tolerance began in England. When Henry VIII's divorce was not recognized by the pope, he decided to be his own "pope" of the Church of England and eventually had six wives, their fates being divorced, beheaded, died, divorced, beheaded, or survived.

His advisers suggested that to solidify his break

with Rome, he should replace the Latin Bible with an English Bible so people there would look to England for their spiritual heritage. Henry did so, but something unexpected happened - people began to read the Bible and compare what was written in it to the king divorcing and beheading his wives.

This group wanted to purify the Church of England, resulting in their nickname, "Puritans." The king did not think he needed purifying, so he persecuted them, resulting in 20,000 Puritans fleeing to Massachusetts, where they tolerated ... only Puritans.

Roger Williams was not tolerated in Massachusetts, so he fled, founding Providence, R.I., and the first Baptist church in America. Thomas Hooker was not tolerated, so he fled, founding Hartford, Conn., and the Congregational Church. The Quakers, considered heretics, were not tolerated and, with leader William Penn, they founded Pennsylvania. Within a generation, tolerance developed for all Protestant denominations.

Another generation went by, and Catholics began to be tolerated. Maryland was the first colony to tolerate Catholics with its Toleration Act; Philadelphia built its first Catholic church in 1731; and in 1776, one of 56 signers of the Declaration of Independence was Catholic, Charles Carroll, who was the richest man in America, and his cousin started Georgetown.

In the early 1800s, French enlightenment thought experienced a period of popularity in New England, and tolerance was extended to "liberal" Christian denominations, such as Unitarians and Universalists, as they quoted from the Bible and called themselves followers of Christ.

The expanding Christian populace decided to promote tolerance of non-Christians, based on Jesus' example of never forcing anyone to believe in him, and that to be pleasing to God, true religion was voluntary from the inside-out, not forced from the outside-in. To fulfill the Great Commission, therefore, those of other faiths should be allowed to come in so they might have an opportunity to hear the Gospel.

Jews experienced varying degrees of tolerance, but it was not until 1851 that Maryland's Constitution was amended to let Jews hold office. In 1860, Morris Jacob Raphall was the first Rabbi ever to open a session of Congress with prayer, and President Lincoln was the first to allow Hebrew chaplains in the military.

In the second half of the 1800s, tolerance was extended to monotheists anyone believing in one God. U.S. coins were inscribed with the National Motto, "In God We Trust," - not "gods." Oaths of office ended with "So Help Me God," - not "gods." A monotheistic God was acknowledged in federal courts, which open with the invocation "God save the United States and this honorable court." Presidents acknowledged God in their Inaugural Addresses, and each of the 50 state constitutions made reference to God.

Many state constitutions forbade citizenship to Chinese, Japanese and other "Mongolian" races, in part because they were polytheists, believing in many gods. In the early 1900s, tolerance began to expand to polytheists and finally believers in any other religion.

Then, in the last half of the 1900s, tolerance went out to atheists, secular humanists and the anti-religious.

Today, the government's World Factbook lists the United States as being 78 percent Christian (52 percent Protestant, 24 percent Catholic, 2 percent Mormon), 1 percent Jewish, 1 percent Muslim, 10 percent other, and 10 percent none. Ten years ago, it listed the country as 84 percent Christian. But back at the time of America's founding, this percentage was well over 90 percent.

America's predominately Christian founders - basing their concept on the Golden Rule from Jesus' Sermon on the Mount, "do unto others as you would have them do unto you," and Jesus' example of never forcing anyone to believe in him - enlarged the circle of tolerance by attempting to find common ground with the newly arrived immigrants and newly invented beliefs.

The problem today is those "not believing" are now demonstrating intolerance to those "believing," as seen by many activist court cases to remove God from the Pledge, prohibit Ten Commandments monuments, erase Judeo-Christian symbols off city seals, stop prayer at school ball games and graduations, ban Boy Scouts and Salvation Army, and censor historical documents. They are, in effect, establishing a State Religion of Atheistic Secular Humanism.

President Reagan, Feb. 25, 1984, stated: "We're told our children have no right to pray in school. Nonsense. The pendulum has swung too far toward intolerance against genuine religious freedom. It is

74

time to redress the balance."

William J. Federer, is a best-selling author and the president of Amerisearch Inc., a publishing company dedicated to researching America's noble heritage He is the author of the new book "Backfired."

These Christian "rebels" had very strong genes. They braved rickety ships to cross the Atlantic for a future unknown in the American wilderness. They left the "comforts" of the known, Europe, the center of civilization at that time, for the wilderness, mountains, deserts and plains of a country full of unfriendly Native Americans fighting to defend their land from these white invaders.

These new settlers in the new world believed that America was just so expansive that one could work the land (which was basically unlimited in supply-again at the expense of the original indigenous peoples), build up the land, build oneself up and serve the Lord without any tyranny from any church or government leader.

This new nation, America, was made up of rebels who were ready to fight for their freedoms, especially freedom of religion and freedom of speech. In 1820, Alexis De Tocqueville wrote in his book "Democracy in America" that America would be the greatest country on Earth because "Americans were a good people and their pulpits were on fire for the Lord." Conversely, De Tocqueville went on to say that America would lose its pre-eminence in the world when its pulpits ceased being on fire for the Lord.

This book was part of the syllabus in American high schools in 1966 when I was a high school senior. Obviously, because of the reference "pulpits on fire for the Lord" the book was removed from the syllabus for reasons of political correctness and the misconstrued "separation of church and state." What Thomas Jefferson meant was not that God should be deleted from any mention, but that there should not be a State Church just as Anglican in England, Lutheran in Germany or Catholic in Rome. People should be free to worship God in any whichever way they wanted. But unfortunately, misguided liberals have misconstrued this to mean that it is an offense to bring God into the public domain.

Again, without trying to be too judgmental, the wimps and the comfortable Europeans stayed in Europe. Those ready to fight for God and their personal freedoms endangered their lives by crossing the Atlantic to the Americas.

But, going back to Europe, it was the Protestant countries of northern Europe, and especially England, Holland and Belgium that most welcomed the Jews from Spain who were allowed to resume their lives as Jews after fleeing the Spanish and Portuguese Inquisitions.

Like I said before, it was Protestant leader Oliver Cromwell who re-invited the Jews to live in England in 1655 after an absence of four and a half centuries from the time of the Catholic expulsion from York in 1140.

This was the legacy of the "Bible-believing" Christians of the Protestant Reformation. And, of course, if this was so in Europe, how much more so was this true in the new colonies of the Americas?

And so there were Jews living in America virtually from Day #1. There had been Jews on the ships with Christopher Columbus who saw sailing into the unknown future as preferable to burning at the stake of the auto-da-fe in Spain.

Many of the early Spanish colonists were conversos pretending to be Christians. But not far behind these Jews came the Spanish Inquisition to ensure that there were no Jewish heresies in the Spanish colonies, even though there were no Moslems anywhere in the Americas and no threat of

Islamic invasion.

So when Jews began to be burned at the stake in Mexico City, the Jews would move northward toward Monterrey. When the Inquisition made it to Monterrey, the Jews went further north into Texas, Colorado, New Mexico, Arizona and California. They always kept their Judaism or Jewish ethnicity a secret and always tried to stay a step ahead of the Church Inquisitors.

Many actually ceased being Jews altogether, but for some reason maintained certain traditions, like not eating pork, by covering mirrors during periods of mourning, and by lighting candles on Friday nights, all done surreptitiously.

Many Jews who had moved to Holland then moved to New Amsterdam which eventually became New York when taken over by the British. The oldest synagogue in the US is in Newport, Rhode Island, founded by Sephardic (Spanish and Portuguese) Jews.

Indeed many Jews moved into the southern colonies including Charleston, South Carolina and Savannah, Georgia. In fact, I once attended a synagogue in Kansas City, Kansas and heard a lecture by a representative of the Jewish War Veterans who said that there were actually even more Jewish soldiers in the Confederate Army during the American Civil War (1861-65) than there were in the northern army. It was even said that when the Jewish officers in the Confederate Army asked the leader of the Confederacy Jefferson Davis for permission to go home for the Jewish High Holy Days, he was reputed to say that the Confederate Army would collapse if all the Jewish officers went home!

It is also a fact that many German Jews immigrated to Texas after Texas won its independence from Mexico in 1824.

Without dwelling too much more on the Jewish role

in early America, there is one piece of history that must be recounted. General George Washington, leading the American colonists in what seemed almost as an impossible battle against England's King George III, entered the Jewish synagogue in Philadelphia on Yom Kippur, 1777, telling the Jews in no uncertain terms that he was desperate for cash, that he could not pay the revolutionary soldiers. He asked the Jews of Philadelphia on the holiest day of the year for Jews, to go home immediately and return to the synagogue with all the gold they could muster. (The Jewish religion forbids the handling of money or gold on Yom Kippur, so this was a big deed for the Jews to do what Washington asked them to do.

Led by Jewish leader Haim Solomon, the Jews returned with what was in those days $30 million in gold bullion. Some say today that would be worth $30 billion. But the fact is that the Jews saved Washington and the American Revolution on that day. By the way, the US Government never repaid the Jews of Philadelphia.

God says in the Bible "I will bless those who bless you and curse those who curse you." (Genesis.12:3 and Numbers 24:9). This has been a guiding rule for the Christians of America who received the Jews as welcomed brothers and sisters from virtually the first day of colonization in the British Americas.

It was now the turn of the Jews to bless George Washington and the American Revolution. And the Jews have blessed America ever since. I believe that there is this symbiotic relationship between the Jews and Christians which has made America the greatest country in the world. And it is clearly to be seen that all those countries that bless the Jews are the most prosperous and happy nations in the world, and conversely, those countries that curse the Jews are most accursed and miserable of all.

So the Jews have always been an integral part of the American people from Day 1. America was always the land of unlimited dreams. If you worked hard, you would be rewarded for your work. You were free to serve God any whichever way you wished and it was no one's business. You built up the land and with it you were built up.

At this point, I would like to tell of an experience I had in Argentina in the summer of 1965. I was sixteen at the time, and my parents wanted to send me back to their "homeland" Argentina. This was the land where my parents were raised, the country which gave sanctuary to my grandparents when they fled the anti-Semitic persecutions of Russia and Poland. I was to spend three months there studying the Spanish language, literature, and history. Instead of spending my summer vacation in New York going to summer camp, working or enjoying the summer free time, my parents registered me for three months as a visiting student in the prestigious Colegio Nacional de Buenos Aires, the high school of Argentina's presidents and leaders. I also had a private guitar teacher three times a week to coach me in classical and Argentine folk music. So I spent my summer vacation studying and working really hard!

It was the morning of August 14, 1965. There was a roar of military jet aircraft flying in formation over my grandfather's house in Buenos Aires. "Was a military takeover in the offing?" I asked my Uncle Raul.

Raul answered me that this was the anniversary of "Argentina's great victory over the British invaders in 1806 and 1807." (It was during these invasions that the British also stole the Malvinas or Falkland Islands from Argentina.)

He continued by telling me that one day, all the Criollas or locally born Argentine women of Buenos Aires, the capital, went on the rampage and poured boiling cooking oil on the proud British troops parading on the streets outside their windows.

According to the tradition, the British troops panicked and fled to their ships in ignominious defeat at the hands of these wild Argentine women.

Raul said, "This should not be a day of national celebration for Argentina. It should be a day of national mourning. Had the British stayed in Argentina and colonized it like they colonized North America, Argentina today could have been one of the richest and most powerful countries on Earth, just like the US and Canada. Instead Argentina became a corrupt almost third world country."

"Because the British fled," Raul continued, "Argentina reverted to its Spanish character of 'piola'. 'Piola' means wise guy or smart aleck. It means being smarter than the next guy and doing your best to outsmart everyone around you. It means that everyone else gets the "short end of the stick". Most importantly it means to stay above everyone else, even if, and especially if you did it in a ingeniously dishonest manner."

Raul stated emphatically, "The Americans rule the world because of their British culture of positivism, honesty and hard work. The Argentines and virtually all of Latin America is based on the Catholic traditions of conquerors, the 'conquistadores' who came to the New World with Christopher Columbus not to settle and build, like the English settlers, but to pillage, murder, rape the women, enslave the Indians and basically leave scorched earth."

Raul concluded with a popular saying in Argentina: "Roban de dia. Crece de noche." This means: The leaders of Argentina steal all day long. And at night while they sleep, everything grows back because Argentina is a country of such greatness and wealth. But everything is for naught because the leadership thinks only of stealing and self-aggrandizement, not the good of the people.

Again, North America, Australia, New Zealand, South Africa, were countries founded and formed by Protestant peoples whose approach was that of building up the land and being built up with the land, of dedication to the common good, and a deep sense of Christianity which later for reasons of political correctness became renamed as "Judeo-Christian" values.

Latin America was shaped by Spanish and Portuguese conquerors that were still fighting a Crusade or holy war in the new world, this time against pagan Indians, whereas in Spain and Portugal they were fighting the Moslems. The lands were to be divided up by the royalty and the wealth was intended to serve the royalty. It was not the idealism of the English speaking settlers more to the North.

It must also be remembered that the Moslems were in the Iberian Peninsula for 760 years and much of the Islamic character of conquest and barbaric behavior must have "rubbed off" on those who were conquered. The Catholics of Spain and Portugal became brutalized by their Moslem conquerors and became just like them if not worse. Whereas the Moslems became more civilized in Spain, the Christians became more barbaric and despised the refined culture of the Judeo-Islamic Spain of 1492.

As a personal observation, I must add that even though I was born in New York, my parents had arrived as immigrants only a year before I was born. The culture in my parents' home was Argentine. The music, the language, the culture and the spirit of my home was Argentine. My parents always taught me to be proud of their being Argentine and that the culture they came from was far superior to that of Elvis Presley, rock & roll, and Coca Cola. This made me different from all my friends in school and in Hebrew school.

When one adds to this the teachings of Hebrew school that all Christians either killed us or hated us, even in America, it became difficult for me if not impossible to love the US. I was torn. I was American born, but I felt like an Argentine.

But these remarks by my Uncle Raul planted the seeds for me later as I matured to understand the fallacies of Hebrew school that all Christians hated us and the fallacy of my parents that American culture and behavior were inferior to that of Argentina. True, there are wonderful aspects to Argentina, its people and its culture, but there is a reason America is the greatest country on Earth.

Another point I wanted to add is that Voltaire, a Frenchman and an avowed atheist said, "I might not agree with what you have to say, but I will defend with my life your right to say it."

Even though Voltaire was an atheist, this remark is truly a symbol of Judeo-Christian Western Civilization. It is part of the democratic ethic adopted by the people of the United States, and by now most of the Western World.

Much of the thinking of Protestant Christians comes from John Calvin (1509-1564) who, himself, was a Frenchman, like Voltaire.

Protestant America was able to learn from Jews and European Christians and utilize their teachings to everyone's benefit. It is only because of this democratic system in America, Canada and the rest of the Anglo-Saxon world in the 17th, 18th, 19th centuries and later in Europe, Latin America, India and parts of Africa that this openness and tolerance of other religions became the law of the land. Democracy took root. It was the US that was the vanguard.

Eventually, the Catholic Church as well as the mainline churches of European countries which had not shown toleration for dissention in Europe opened up branches in the US and Canada and learned to reform themselves. The terrible Inquisition which burned Protestants alongside Jews in the auto-da-fe ended in the early 1800's. Today throughout the Americas and Europe Catholics and Protestants can live side by side without slaughtering each other except for the occasional terrorism in Northern Ireland.

European Christians have also learned after centuries of mass slaughter of fellow Europeans, that all of this killing was in vain. The purpose of the Common Market, followed later by the European Union, was that it was crazy for White, Christian Europeans to slaughter each other. Today, it is virtually unthinkable for one European nation to go to war against another. This is also a fulfillment of Isaiah: Nation shall not lift up sword against another nation, neither shall men learn war any more. But it is also modern Judeo-Christian Western Civilization which brought this about.

I wanted to conclude this chapter with another aspect of America's greatness. Having lived the first 19 years of my life in New York, I know that most Americans are consumed with only that which directly affects their lives in the US. I was always good in history and geography. Most Americans show a disdain for history and anything outside the borders of the United States. Americans are isolationist by nature. They don't want to get involved in foreign wars that have nothing to do with them.

Americans feel secure. They have the Atlantic Ocean on one side and the Pacific Ocean on the other. Canada, probably the best neighbor the United States could want is to the North and Mexico, another Christian country to the South.

When World War I broke in Europe in 1914, the American people wanted nothing to do with this war. It was a foreign war in a far away place: Europe. A Serbian nationalist killed

Austrian Archduke Ferdinand leading to a declaration of war on Serbia by Austria. Russia was allied with Serbia. Germany was allied with Austria. Britain and France were allied with Russia so they joined to. All this happened because of an assassination.

Why in Heaven's name would America involved itself in such a crazy war? So America remained neutral for more than three years of this war. But in November 1917, an American ocean liner the "Lusitania" was torpedoed off the coast of Ireland. In addition there were secret telegraph transmissions between Germany and Mexico promising the Mexicans that if they supported the Axis Powers, then Mexico would be supported in fighting the United States and retaking the Western territories the US took from Mexico in the war of 1846.

It was America's entry into WWI which basically tipped the scales for the Allies against the Axis Powers and brought an end to WWI.

WWII again was a European and Asian war. The American people were against having anything to do with this war. It wasn't until the Japanese launched their sneak attack on Pearl Harbor on December 7th, 1941, that the American people decided to defend itself by going to war.

By wars end, the destruction was so terrible that the United States helped to rebuild Europe with the Marshall Plan including the aggressor country Germany and its General Douglas McArthur who rebuilt Japan, the other aggressor country. America was magnanimous in victory. America basically saved the world from the tyranny of Nazi Germany and Tojo's Japan.

Immediately after WWII began the Cold War with Communism and Soviet Russia. Again, it was America which almost singlehandedly saved the world and defeated

Communism in 1989.

There is no other country in the world that could save the world in WWI, WWII, and the Cold War, and yet everyone resents America. That is until people from the world over decide to move to America.

Then came the events of 9/11. It was only America that could lead in the battle against Islamic terrorism, and yet the world still hates America.

I have come to the conclusion that the same hatred the anti-Semites bear toward the Jews is identical to the hatred of the world toward the United States. Causeless, baseless hatred.

But the world would not be free today were it not for the United States. The prosperity of the world is also directly linked to the prosperity of the United States. If the United States takes a direct hit from Islamic terrorism causing a collapse of the American economy, the whole world will suffer. Millions will starve.

The United States is the world's vanguard. Nazi Germany was vanquished and Judeo-Christian Western Civilization and Democracy replaced that terrible totalitarian system. Tojo's Japan was replaced by a democratic Japan. Even the former republics of the Soviet Socialist Bloc are now thirsting for freedom and democracy.

Latin America which used to be dominated by military dictatorships is now free and democratic. The only dictatorship in the Western Hemisphere is that of Communist Cuba and Fidel Castro. But this Cuban dinosaur will end its days as well replaced by democracy.

Only Democracy works. We are left with the Communist countries of China, North Korea and Cuba, the last holdouts, but they, too, are dinosaurs. Their systems inevitably will be replaced by democracy.

This leaves only the Islamic world. Since Islam is the antithesis of democracy, it will be interesting to see if and how democracy takes root in countries like Iraq, Afghanistan and Lebanon.

The days of Islamic despotism are numbered. Islam must be terminated. As Churchill said, "Democracy is a terrible system, but all the other systems are so much worse." And I will add, "Islam is the worst of all the worse systems."

CHAPTER FIVE

Globalism

In Chapters II and III, I discussed the Five Deceptions of Islam and the Islamic Invasions, Past, Present and Future, or Islam and its fruits of evil.

In Chapter IV, I very feebly attempted to summarize the anti-dote to the Islamic Threat to humanity: Judeo-Christian Western Civilization and Democracy. It is my humble belief that God created the United States as a counterbalance to the evils of Islam as well as Nazism and Communism. All three systems are threats to humanity.

However, in Chapter V, I want to discuss Globalism, after Islam, the second greatest threat to Israel's existence and to those promises made by God to Israel as stipulated in the Bible. This will show another reason why Israel's Bible Bloc Party is such a must. Globalism is another system threatening the Judeo-Christian West.

I think it is fair to say that there are two types of human beings: those who believe in ideologies and those who believe only in money.

Ideologies include Nazism, Communism, and all religions. They require altruism and idealism from their followers. Capital, money, or wealth is a tool to be used for the loftier purpose.

Then there are people who believe in money as their ideology. That anyone or anything may be purchased with money, that there are no ideologies any more.

When people like former president of the US Bill Clinton says: "Hey, it's the economy, stupid!" he is denying the existence of God, through whom all wealth is attained (Deuteronomy 8).

When the former secretary of state of the US, Colin Powell says that the key to the Palestinian refugee problem is money, that it is poverty that creates terrorism, he totally overlooks Islam (religion & ideology) as a factor.

When former prime minister of Israel Shimon Peres says he will create a "New Middle East" turning Israel and its Arab neighbors into a Middle East Common Market, he is denying the existence of two conflicting ideologies: Islam and Judeo-Christian Western Civilization and Democracy for the fallacy that money can straighten everything out. He is dead wrong.

One of the first purposes of this chapter is to straighten out those people who read this book who think that it's all about money. By the way, most of the 19 homicide-bombers of 9/11 came from relatively well-to-do families. They were not lacking money. They were motivated by ideology. They were motivated by Islam.

But the main purpose of this chapter is to show that leaders, both democratic and republican, in Washington, DC are so corrupted by their rapacious appetites for wealth that if the wealth is from the Islamic oil world, and this Islamic oil world calls for the destruction of Israel, these so-called "Christian" leaders will buckle under gladly for the profits they expect to make from the Moslems even if it means the destruction of Israel and Jerusalem by the Moslems.

Because, after all: Hey it's the economy stupid. And then there are those pastors who are considered Christian but go along with this for self-serving reasons. And then there are those Jews, as well, who see money as their god and not the God of Abraham, Isaac, and Jacob and his promises to Israel and those who bless Israel.

Now, on the one hand, in Chapter IV, I praised the United States and believed that God created the US as a counterbalance to the forces of evil. But today, meaning in the last few decades, we see a United States that for reasons of economic and political "wisdom" sacrificed six million Jews in WWII to the gas chambers for reasons I will review later on in this book and now is forcing Israel to withdraw from lands that belong to the Jews by God's promises in the Bible. These "compromises" Israel is being forced to make by the World, led by America could, God-forbid, lead to Israel's destruction. It is the financial leverage or pressure of petroleum and the almighty "Petrodollar" (mostly in the hands of the Islamic paymasters) that is seeking to crush Israel.

The following testimony I want to share is one that I have repeated in all three of my previous books. It remains the primary reason for my work and for the vision I have of a Judeo-Christian political party in the Knesset in Jerusalem as well as an international Judeo-Christian alliance.

For those people who know me and my message, it is the testimony of the Dallas Council on World Affairs of April 1991.

It is always a shock for me when I meet up with Jewish brethren who hate the Christians. I dealt with this from the beginning of this book. They love the Moslems for the myth that it was good under the Moslems. They hate the Christians, all Christians, for the myth that all Christians were bad to us.

I used to be like that: "Been there, done that!"

When I first started speaking to Christian churches and audiences in November 1990, I still was of that mindset, myself, though willing maybe, to give the Christians half a chance. I had been fired illegally in October 1990 from the Prime Minister's Office (under Yitzhak Shamir) was blocked from any really good employment for which I was qualified by lies placed in my file by socialist bureaucrats, and frankly, when the door opened in the US to start speaking up about Israel's message, I realized that this was an important window opening for me in the US when all the windows had closed for me in Israel.

Would I have ever considered leaving my wife and children in Israel for up to eight months of the year in order to drive around the US, Canada and Europe had I been offered a good employment in Israel? And this has been my life since 1990.

There are two women in Texas who played a role in my life and work. One was Christian, the other Jewish.

Nancy, the Christian lady had been corresponding with me by mail since 1986. When I was fired illegally at the Government Press Office, Nancy said to me "Ya'll come down to Texas and I will get you to speak in churches, synagogues, radio and TV." And that's what she indeed did.

In November 1990, I was in Texas speaking in the churches and synagogues that Nancy set up, and one day she said to me: "A door has opened. Tonight there is going to be a fund-raiser for KVTT Christian radio in Dallas. Marlin Maddoux, a famous radio talk show host for the "Point of View" program will be hosting. If he meets you, he will have you on his show!"

I told Nancy that it was a long shot, but we would try. So we drove five hours from San Antonio to Dallas and got to the dinner late, but just in time to meet with Marlin Maddoux. The next morning, he interviewed me on his show. I have been doing radio shows with "Point of View" ever since. Our hosts for this fundraiser were Evelyn and Eric Gustavson, from Cleburne, Texas. I will return to them in a moment.

Now Nancy also spoke to Rabbi Richard Spiegel, the then rabbi of Agudas Achim, the local Conservative synagogue in San Antonio. He had never heard of me, since I was relatively unknown and new on the lecture circuit, but he invited me to speak since it was November 1990, just two months before Operation Desert Storm which began on January 16th, 1991.

Since a family was celebrating the Bar Mitzvah of its son, that Sabbath in the synagogue, many out of town guests came including a Jewish woman, Elizabeth (Rusty) Robertson, owner of a well-known PR Agency in Dallas. After my message, she came up to me and said: "You need to speak before the "Dallas Council on World Affairs. I will arrange it for you."

When I returned to the United States for my second lecture circuit visit in April 1991, just after the end of Operation Desert Storm, I received a call from Rusty Robertson to get on the next plane and come down to Dallas because I was to speak before the Dallas Council on World Affairs the very next day!

Now, I did not understand this at the time, but my host at the Dallas Council was a General Latham. He told me that Russia's Boris Yeltsin had been contracted to give four lectures to the Council. Yeltsin indeed gave two of the four lectures but then got so drunk that he had to be placed on a stretcher and flown back to Moscow to a sanatorium because of his alcoholism. So the Dallas Council, which had already committed itself to the four meetings at the exclusive

91

"Stouffer Hotel," now needed a speaker. I was the speaker. Boris Yeltsin had to be so drunk that he couldn't speak so that I could.

By the way, my former boss at the Government Press Office in Jerusalem, Mr. Yoram Ettinger, was at this time Israel Embassy's head of relations with the conservative members of Congress in Washington. Ettinger congratulated me on being invited to speak to this prestigious group in Dallas. He asked me, "How did you arrange this meeting for yourself? We have been trying for years to get one of our official representatives in to speak, but so far, unsuccessfully!"

It bears mentioning that relations between the Yitzhak Shamir government in Jerusalem and the George Herbert Walker Bush administration in Washington DC were not good to say the least. Being a stalwart Likud supporter and speaking to the Dallas Council on World Affairs was a miracle to say the least!

By the way, General Latham received me so warmly in Dallas that I felt like a general in the Israeli Army. Indeed, one of his first questions to me was: "So, General Lipkin, what is it like to be a general in the Israeli army?"

Totally astonished, I replied: "General? I am Lieutenant (reserves) Avi Lipkin of the Israel Defense Forces Spokesman's Office. He thought that the guest who flew down from New York with 24 hour notice was General Amnon Lipkin Shahak, former chief of staff of the IDF. But now it was too late to cancel me as the speaker because the people were already in the conference hall waiting for their "general" to speak.

And indeed, General Latham introduced me as "General Avi Lipkin." I wasn't going to protest and embarrass him.

My message, though, was indeed a professional military message. I knew that politics was a hot potato, because of the poor relations between Shamir and Bush the father, so I stuck to the professional military message. By the way, amongst the some odd 200 people in attendance, about 20 were Arabs, very rich Arabs. All the people there that night were very rich. All you need to do was look at how they were dressed.

So I knew all eyes were on me, (and even those of my former boss Yoram Ettinger at the Israeli Embassy in Washington DC) and I needed to provide these most important VIP people of Dallas with a top notch IDF Spokesman's presentation that even Arabs could listen to and not walk out. By the way, these people of the Dallas Council on World Affairs were part of the famous or infamous Council on Foreign Relations. These are the people who control the economy of the United States and the World. These are faceless people behind the scenes who decide who the president of the United States will be as well as leaders of other countries. I could feel the power these people had.

They control the banks, corporations, and oil companies that control the world.

This was a night that changed my life forever.

My message was a simple message. Israeli military strategy is non-political. But it must include contingency plans for the two major threats facing Israel's existence.

One strategy is the classic military doctrine of: whoever controls the borders controls the security of the country. Infantry, artillery, tanks and air force cannot defend a country if the borders are indefensible. Therefore, borders are the key. This is basically the approach of the Likud and right-wing parties in Israeli politics.

The other strategy, especially in light of Desert Storm and the 39 Scuds Iraqi Dictator Saddam Hussein launched at Israel from January to March of 1991 taught Israel's military a lesson that missiles do not stop at borders. Borders no longer ensured a country's security. Peace did. All the Arabs needed was four nuclear tipped missiles hitting Israel's four major cities and no more Israel. This is the approach of the Israel's Labor and left-wing parties.

So I steered clear of the politics of Israel and tried to show that the Israeli Army had to maintain aloof from politics and because of the vicissitudes of Israeli politics, to be ready for either of the two military doctrines: Classic and Missile.

I also explained that it takes only three minutes to fly a military jet attack aircraft from Amman, Jordan to Jerusalem, and another three minutes to reach Tel-Aviv. Since "scramble time" in the US Air Force is eleven minutes, that means Israel must always have its aircraft airborne to meet any potential air attack.

I also explained that it takes twenty minutes to drive up from the Jordanian border at the Dead Sea and reach Jerusalem. Commandos could jog up to Jerusalem in five hours. That was the classic doctrine. Israel's border had to remain at the Jordan River.

Similarly, Syria's military aircraft could take off and hit Tiberias in 3 minutes and Haifa in six. Syrian soldiers on the Sea of Galilee would be able to march on Tiberias in 20 minutes, Nazareth in two hours and Haifa in six hours. Therefore, Israel had to maintain its control of the Golan Heights.

My explanation was simple. Any withdrawal from the present borders (1991) would leave Israel totally defenseless. If the Dutch boy pulled his finger out of the dike, the whole region would be flooded. If Israel were to withdraw from its 1991 borders, the Golan Heights, the Jordan River or Gaza, Israel would not be able to defend itself from invaders entering from Egypt, Jordan or Syria.

At the same time, I reminded my august audience that Israel had been attacked again and again and again in 1948, 56, 67, 68-70, and 73. In the 67 and 73 wars, Israel expanded because of Arab wars of aggression. In response, the United Nations passed Resolutions 242 and 338 calling on Israel to hand over "land for peace." And indeed, Israel handed over half the Golan in June 1974 as part of the Kissinger-led Syrian-Israeli Disengagement Talks. This represented 2% of the lands Israel was forced to take in wars of self-defense. In 1981, Israel handed over every last grain of sand of the Sinai Peninsula to Egypt for peace. Sinai represented 91% of the lands Israel was forced to take in wars of self-defense.

Since UN Resolutions 242 and 338 spoke of Israel negotiating with its Arab neighbors for "new borders which were secure, recognized and defensible", and since Israel had already fulfilled a handover of 93% of the lands, I contended that the remaining 7%: the Golan, the Jordan River border and Gaza were and are essential to Israel's defense. Any movement in retreat would mean breaching the dam holding back the waters of Islamic aggression to wipe Israel off the face of the Earth.

That was my message. It was a good message. But more importantly was what I was about to hear after the dinner. We had just finished eating, and I was preparing to leave thinking that I had completed my task for that evening.

General Latham said to me, "No, we're not finished with you yet! We still have questions and answers."

So, I entered a much smaller room with only about 20 people seated around a big square table. These were the crème de la crème of Dallas, oil people, bankers, ranchers and corporation CEO's.

Also seated to my right and left were the Gustavson's who arranged for me to be on the Marlin Maddoux radio show six months before. Eric and Evelyn sat to my left and Carol, their daughter and her husband, Dr. Burton sat to my right.

I was unprepared for what was about to happen. One of these Dallas Council people said to me, "Avi, you are a good spokesman for Israel. This is because you are American born. You don't speak with a 'funny Israeli accent'. We can understand everything you're saying. Your Israeli Government sends us people with funny accents. Now, here in Dallas, we don't like funny accents (sic). We don't like Russian accents (Yeltsin), Arabic accents (from the many oil people and potentates they hosted), Jewish accents (from Israel) and even Oxford English accents – and you speak like a NY Yankee! But you speak clearly. So you are a good spokesman for Israel.

"But you don't know realities. We, here, of the Dallas Council on World Affairs are going to teach you realities.

"First reality: America is tired of paying for your wars. Israel is going to make peace with the Palestinians whether it likes it or not. We don't care if you've already handed over to the Arab side 93% of the lands you took in your wars. You're going to hand over not 93%, or 97%, but 100% and more! You Israelis are all alone. And we don't even care about UN Resolutions 242 and 338 calling for new borders which are recognized and defensible.

"Second reality: There is only one thing that made America great: the barrel of oil - the steady price of oil, the steady supply of oil. Is that clear?"

Now, of course, I was new to this entire lecture circuit milieu, and definitely high level meetings with well-oiled politicians. I was in shock.

Meanwhile, seated next to me was Eric Gustavson, my Christian patron from Cleburne, Texas seated at my side. He

96

was shaking like a tuning fork. He stood up and asked for permission to speak. It was granted. What he said changed my life.

"You call yourselves Christians?" he asked. "You say that what made America great was the barrel of oil? You should be ashamed of yourselves! What made America great was not the barrel of oil. What made America great was Jesus Christ!"

Then his daughter, Carol Burton, stood up asking for permission to address the group: "Besides, it says in the Bible 'Those who bless Israel are blessed, and those who curse Israel are cursed." And she sat down.

Now, finally, I got my thoughts together and stood up to respond. "You know, we Jews never came in the way of America's oil supplies. In fact we paid for your oil supplies with six million of our people in WWII. When the Arabs and their oil snapped the whip in the 1930's and 1940's, the US and Britain decided to not give the Jews seeking to flee from Nazi Europe visas to Palestine, England, the Western Hemisphere or wherever. It is true that Hitler and the Nazis physically killed the Jews, but the decision to industrially liquidate the Jews in gas chambers was only taken in January 1942 at the Wannese Conference in Berlin because there were now over 7 million Jews holed up in ghettos behind Wehrmacht lines and the world would not grant the Jews asylum. So we Jews were massacred so as not to get in the way of the Arab oil. Breckenridge Long, US Under-Secretary of State for visas made sure to it that no Jews would get visas to get into the US, Canada or Cuba.

There was even the famous story of the German passenger liner "St. Louis" which departed from the German sea port of Hamburg in May 1939 with over 900 German Jewish refugees on board. They had valid German passports

97

and valid visas to Cuba. But when the St. Louis arrived in the Port of Havana, it turns out that Washington, DC under Breckenridge Long instructed the Cuban government to revoke the Cuban visas and send the ship back to Germany.

No one was let off the ship, not even the children. The ship turned around and stopped off the coast of Palm Beach, Florida. The US Coast Guard made sure to it that no Jews could "jump ship". The ship then continued to Canada, but the then Prime Minister of Canada McKenzie King also refused to grant asylum to even one person from the ship. The Baptists submitted petitions to President Roosevelt to at least let the children off the ship as a humanitarian gesture but to no avail. The ship returned to Nazi Germany where over 800 of the 900 refugees died in Nazi concentration camps. So the Jews were the price for steady oil prices and supplies.

"And now you mean to say that it is going to happen again?" I asked. "You guys are going to sacrifice five million more Jews in Israel for the barrel of oil?" The answer was affirmative. Israel would be sacrificed for a barrel of oil, meaning Holocaust II.

All of a sudden, "the lights went on." Here I was, an American Jew from New York who was from 1968 to 1991 living in Israel and serving in the Israeli military reserves, coming to America to explain Israel's position to the American people. Until that night in April 1991, I went from hating Christians to really just not liking them so much. But when Eric Gustavson said: "What made America great was not the barrel of oil, but Jesus Christ" I fell in love with these Christians because I finally understood who the enemy was and who my ally was.

It was the globalists who would sacrifice me, my wife, my family and my people Israel for a barrel of oil. It was the Christians who would make their stand with us, and all of this in the name of their savior. Now, of course, until that night, I hated Jesus of Nazareth. I hated Christians, I hated churches and everything that had represented for me 2,000 years of Christian persecution. But that night, the lights went on. I finally realized that out there were tens of millions if not hundreds of millions of Christians that loved Israel and put Jerusalem at the top of their list of joys. The Christians weren't our best friends. They were our only friends.

As a follower of Likud Prime Minister Yitzhak Shamir, it became clear to me that Israel needed to do more to mobilize these Christians so that Israel would survive the threat of Islam joined by these globalist oil company/bank/corporation people who saw Israel as the "fly in the ointment" that had to be destroyed for global economic order. I saw the deaths of six million Jews before me and that history was about to repeat itself.

But maybe if the Christians were mobilized and would stand with Israel, then maybe, just maybe we could have the victory over 1.3 billion Moslems and their rich allies who control the entire world.

So as a Jew, I had to make a decision: Do I continue to hate Jesus of Nazareth, or do I change my tune. How can I work with the Christians if I hate their messiah who just happens to be a Hebrew speaking Jew from Israel?

Do I continue to align myself with the liberals such as President Franklin Delano Roosevelt, who made sure to it that six million Jews were refused visas and therefore were killed in the Holocaust? or do I align myself with these "redneck" Bible believing Christians throughout America who are so reviled by the liberal Jews, 85% of these Jews never having stepped foot on Israeli soil, because most of these Jews don't really care very much about Israel's existence.

Had America had a truly Christian president during WWII, perhaps the six million or at least the vast majority of them could have been saved from death. But it was the liberals and the globalists who made sure to it that the European Jews died, and were now seeking another Holocaust of the Jews and everyone else living in the Holy Land – all for a barrel of oil.

It was that night in April 1991 that I realized that Israel's failure to mobilize the Christians is a major strategic failure that had to be corrected. And I in my own modest way intended to do something about it. But until this day, the Israeli Foreign Ministry, civil service, and establishment are controlled by "liberals" and "socialists" who hate the born again Bible believing Christians who stand with Israel because of the godlessness of liberal and socialist Jews. I will deal with this in Chapter VI.

The Talmud forbids Jews from speaking in churches. But if that is what it takes to mobilize tens of millions or hundreds of millions of Christians worldwide to march for Zion's sake, I will break that commandment.

And if in order to reach the Christians on their own wave length, I need to study the New Testament in spite of the Talmud forbidding me from doing so, I will break that commandment as well.

And if I must read the Koran and Hadith in order to understand my enemy I will do so. And by the way, if any Jew reads both the Christian New Testament and the Islamic Koran, there is no doubt that that Jew will come to the inescapable conclusion that the Christian teachings are allied with our teachings while the Islamic teachings teach the destruction of the Jew on Saturday and the Christian on Sunday. But since the Talmud was written a hundred years before the times of Mohammed, the Talmud provides absolutely no solutions to this problem of Nazi-Islamo-Fascist plans to destroy all human beings who don't convert to Islam.

I want to share another striking testimony I received in a church in the American Pacific Northwest. For security reasons, I will delete certain details in order not to compromise the security of the pastor who shared this with me.

When this pastor heard my testimony about the Dallas Council on World Affairs, he insisted on telling me his story. He had been a sailor in the US Navy in the late 70's and early 80's. Because of some heroic deed he performed, the captain of the ship decided to promote him to officer training, but before he could be promoted, the pastor (who was then just a sailor) had to pass something known as the "loyalty test."

The captain asked him: "If you were captain of this ship, what would you do if you were given orders to 'nuke' Tel Aviv?" (By the way, we're not talking about a Soviet ship, an Arab or Islamic ship. We are talking about a US ship nuking Israel!)

The pastor (sailor) answered with a laugh.

"Why are you laughing?" asked the captain.

He answered, "Because I am a Christian. God would never allow Israel to be nuked. It says so in the Bible. And secondly, I wouldn't want to be on that ship. God would take out that ship and its nuclear weapon if it really tried to attack Israel."

The sailor never became an officer. He failed the "loyalty exam" but he passed God's exam.

By the way, the captain was promoted to a very senior position in the US Navy before he retired. Today the former captain works for a Saudi company. So people capable of pressing the atomic weapon buttons on US Navy ships eventually get jobs for the Saudis. Scary, Scary!

So the lines have been drawn. The Globalists are people for whom money is their god. They will sacrifice the Jews, the blacks in Africa in the millions, and even their own Christians for a barrel of oil. Globalist Christians like those of the Dallas Council on World Affairs are not really Christians. And Jews who are globalists would also sacrifice Israel for the barrel of oil. They are not really Jews, either.

The inspiration for my second book: "Christian Revival for Israel's Survival" was specifically for that purpose. Here the victims were Christians from Serbia.

In the 1990's, there were two major wars in the Balkans with the breakup of Yugoslavia. Serbia, the predominant of six republics comprising Yugoslavia ended up relinquishing Slovenia almost without a fight. But then Serbia lost Croatia after some battles including the area known as Kraina which had always been settled by the Serbs.

But it was the war in Bosnia, later followed by the loss of Kosovo to ethnic Albanians that was never explained to the Americans and especially the Christians.

Most Americans know little about the Balkans and care even less. It is a small seemingly insignificant corner of southeastern Europe. Why should anyone care?

But the fact is, in spite of the excesses that the Serbs, Croatians, and Moslems all committed against each other, the simple fact is that the cards were stacked against the Serbs because the One World Globalist movement was on the side of the Moslems and Catholic Slovenians and Croatians, while the Serbs were Serbian Orthodox.

So Christians from the West, from Europe and the US, from NATO, went to war against the Serbs in order to take Christian land away and give it to the Moslems. And if Christians (who are ignorant of Balkan history) can take Christian land away and give it to the Moslems, then they

102

can definitely do it the Jews in Israel as well!

This is because the globalist allegiance is with money and oil something the Moslems have and the Serbs don't have.

In Africa, millions of blacks including Africans who are Muslims have been and are at present being slaughtered by the whiter Moslems of North Africa. Why is the world silent? because the Islamic agenda is untouchable. The Moslems have the oil and money. Blacks may be and are being slaughtered with impunity.

In Indonesia, over half a million ethnic Chinese were slaughtered in the 60's by the Moslems, and the world remained silent. In 1975, the Indonesia army marched into East Timor and 300,000 Catholics were slaughtered – 30% of that population.

And have we forgotten the million and a half Armenians slaughtered by the Turks in WWI? Even Hitler said: "Because the world said nothing about the Armenian Holocaust, no one would say anything about the Jewish Holocaust."

So I learned that my allegiance would be to the Bible believing Christians and not to the liberals so that my country Israel would have better chances of surviving. Most Jews unfortunately in Israel, the US and globally still have this "knee-jerk" reaction to the Christians for what the Catholic and Eastern Orthodox churches did during 2,000 years to the Jews.

But today, it is the Protestant Bible believing Christians, or at least some of them, of the last five hundred years who make up the vanguard of those Christians who would give their lives for Israel to survive, whereas the "liberal" Christians and most of their mainline churches would "look the other way" as they did during the Nazi Holocaust.

Therefore, it is incumbent upon us as Jews and Christians

to learn from the mistakes of history and after 2,000 years of "bad blood" finally start loving each other and working together to save Israel, the US and the World from the threat of Islam and its rapacious oil/money allies.

CHAPTER SIX

Socialism – Israel's Third Threat

In the previous chapters, I spoke of Islam and Globalism as primary threats to Israel's existence. These are external threats. But there is a third threat, an internal one: that of Socialism. It is a force which created Israel out of the deserts, bare mountains and swamps that comprised Ottoman and British Palestine. It was the "booster" rocket which got Israel off to a start in the first place. But all along, from day one, there was a price to pay for Socialism and today the price has become so onerous that like a booster rocket on a missile, eventually it must be discarded, and replaced by Judeo-Christian Western Civilization and Democracy. Until then, Socialism is a threat to Israel, the third threat.

Firstly, in order to review the birth and growth of Socialism worldwide, I think it fair to relate a few personal autobiographical details. Again, so much of this book is: "Been there, done that."

I was born into a family and grew up in a home where there was much disdain for Socialism. My parents' families originally from in Poland and Russia were very religious until the time came for them to flee to the New World – America. Eventually, because of their being new immigrants in

105

Argentina and their struggle to feed themselves, the religion became a thing of the past, a burden too grievous to be born. In addition, there was not very much of an organized Jewish community in Argentina during the first half of the twentieth century.

My parents knew that they were Jewish, but that was all. My parents always respected our Judaism, but knew nothing of it. When they left Argentina for the US, and I grew up in New York, my parents decided to provide me with a Jewish education, something they could never have. As our family's economic situation stabilized and improved in the United States, my parents' approach was conservative politically as well as religiously. We became members in a Conservative synagogue in New York.

By the way, I referred in Chapter I to my mother's teaching me about the greatness of Spain in our Jewish as well as world history. But there is also another story to be told. When the Spanish Civil War broke out in 1936, my mother joined the Argentine branch of the Spanish Republican Party and was just about to volunteer to go off to Spain to join the Socialist International Brigade and to fight the Fascist Dictator General Francisco Franco.

It was then that she met my father. My father gave her an ultimatum: Choose between my father and Franco. So my father made short shrift of my mother's Socialist inclinations. A short time after my mother left the Socialist Republicans in Argentina, that group was raided by the Argentine police and incarcerated. Fortunately my mother came out of this Socialist adventure unscathed.

By the way, another historical footnote about General Franco: When my wife's family in Egypt underwent the terrible persecutions that took place in Egypt during the Six Day War and in its aftermath, it was the Spanish Government under Franco which granted passports to my wife's family because of their Spanish heritage. No other government would help the "stateless" Jews of Egypt. My father-in-law was incarcerated for two years simply because he was a Jew. All Jewish men in Egypt were jailed on the first day of the Six Day War. So thanks to the Fascist Dictator Franco, my wife and her family received passports and protection from Spain.

Indeed there is a tradition that Francisco Franco, himself, had Jewish blood and was descended from people who were once Jewish. It is also a fact that Franco sent his ambassadors in Europe into the Nazi concentration camps to seek out Jews of Hispanic ancestry and saved at least 70,000 Jews from the gas chambers. So the Fascist Franco ended up saving more Jews in WWII than the liberal US President Franklin Delano Roosevelt!

During the Viet Nam War, I was already studying in college at New York University, Washington Square College, and saw all around me the anti-war protesters who were preaching free love, pot, civil disobedience and of course, Socialism. My immediate knee-jerk reaction was a severe allergy to this kind of thinking.

In fact when I was part of the student body at New York University and had to judge two young students who were caught shoplifting and then at the police station found to be in possession of drugs, I demanded that these two young ladies be expelled from Weinstein Dormitory because I considered them a "sick element". The immediate reaction of my peers: "You are Fascist." Boy, oh boy, are the Fascists racking up points in my book! If being against drugs makes me a Fascist, so be it!

I decided, from my very limited exposure to life in America because of my experience of living only in the New

York area that all of America was sick, very sick and that America was like the Titanic, sinking fast in the immorality, drug abuse and loss of the traditional values of the founding fathers that made America great. I did not yet have exposure to the "moral majority" in America's hinterland. That was to come twenty years later.

Therefore, it was in 1968 that I left America and moved to Israel. Israel had just had the stunning victory in 1967 of the Six Day War. It controlled immense territory it did not have before June 5th, 1967, including Jerusalem, Judea, Samaria, the Golan, Gaza and Sinai. There was euphoria in Israel of victory and a growing homeland. There was not this feeling of purposelessness, defeat, and the sickness of the Socialist left as I perceived it in the United States.

In 1964, I had joined the Betar Youth Movement and was proud to continue my membership upon making Aliyah or moving to Israel in August, 1968. It was on January 14th 1970 that I met my wife, Rachel, and as I mentioned in Chapter I, she was on a bus with these virulent Communists and Socialists who had just fled from military dictatorships in Argentina, Brazil, Chile and Uruguay.

This was the period known as the "ugly war". These students could have "disappeared" had they stayed home in South America. Their parents wanted to save their children from disappearing off the streets and being killed by the Fascist military regimes in those countries at that time. So they ended up in Israel. By the way after their cursing me that day on the bus, we all became best of friends!

So, dear reader, you may ask: "Who is a Socialist, and who is a Fascist?" Why do I believe Socialism to be a threat to Israel?

It is not my purpose to give a long extended history of Fascism and Socialism nor am I able to. But there are a few relevant facts from my life's experiences I would like to share which shed light on this questions and on which I base this book.

Fascism and Socialism are ideologies that developed in the 1800's in Europe in almost every country of Europe and later throughout the world. They developed especially in those countries where democracy was absent: in the Germanic nations, Italy, and the East European countries.

These two ideologies were secular in nature and in the case of Fascism, grew alongside and sometimes in partnership with the churches of those countries.

Fascism comes from the Italian word Fascio which means fastening rope, such as binds a sheaf of wheat in the field. The Fascio keeps the wheat together. It "unifies" and galvanizes the people to reach the goals of the nation and prevents anarchy.

In the case of Italy, the idea was that all the individual kingdoms be unified into one country. This was the accomplishment of Garibaldi in 1861.

In the case of Germany, it was Bismarck who united all these little Germanic kingdoms into Prussia and later Germany by 1870.

In the Slavic areas of Europe, it was the Catholic Church that delineated the ethnic definition of the Croats, Slovenians, Poles, Czechs, Slovaks and Ukrainians. Islam was the religion of the Bosnians, Albanians and ethnic Turks of Greece and Bulgaria. Eastern Orthodox Christianity was the religion of the Serbs, Greeks, Bulgarians, Romanians, and Russians. All the nationalisms of all these groups were based on their religious affiliations.

Then there was Socialism. Marx and Engels, originally of Jewish background, but who were secular, felt that the solution for the world's problems was to do away with religions and ethnic backgrounds altogether and to unite the whole world under the banner of atheism or at least secularism. Of course, being Jewish by birth, they felt the brunt of all these anti-Semitic Church and nationalist persecutions. The best way, they thought, to bring peace on Earth was to provide economic and political equality to all human beings, and Socialism for them was the way. Communist is an offshoot of Socialism, but even more radical seeking to collectivize all wealth under the control of the Communist Party which was usually about 1% of the population.

Everyone was equal, but the 1% that controlled was more equal than the 99%.

Now, getting back to some autobiographical details, I considered myself a Zionist and also a patriotic American defending Western Democracy from the threat of Communism/Socialism during the Cold War which included the Viet Nam War. This was merely a war by proxy between the US and Russia.

In 1966 as a freshman at college, I decided that to defeat the enemy, Communism, one needed to learn about it. My feeling in life is, when you have an enemy you must learn about the enemy either to defeat it or befriend it. One cannot defeat an enemy nor befriend a former enemy until getting to know that enemy. Interestingly also for me, there was always this ambivalence between opposing the enemy and falling in love with its people, history, culture and aspirations.

Indeed in that college period at New York University of 1966-68, I saw Russia as the adversary, but I fell in love with the language, culture, music and history of the Russian people. But I did study the ideology of Communism and saw a bankrupt, corrupt system that was the ruination not only of Russia, but of all the nations that fell under Communist domination. Communism destroyed its own people just as

110

Nazism destroyed the Germans in WWII.

Then there was Socialism, a slightly milder malady but also not very friendly to the US, or the West, and definitely not toward my new adopted country Israel.

In fact, when I moved to Israel in 1968, many fellow Jews and Israelis warned me: If you are a member of the "rightwing" Betar, you will never be able to get a job in Israel. All employment in Israel is controlled by the Socialist leftist government of Israel. It would behoove me, they said, to switch allegiances, get a red membership card from the Socialist Histadrut Labor Movement and even join the Labor Party. That's the way it was in the Communist/Socialist countries of Eastern Europe, Communist China, North Korea and Indo-China. The same applied to Socialist Israel. Either you are part of the Israeli Socialist Establishment or you are nothing.

But I stuck with the Betar Youth Movement and its Israeli political outgrowth, the Herut Party of Menahem Begin. Later Herut became Gahal (Herut-Liberals) in 1966 and in 1973 it became the Likud Party.

To understand Socialism in Israel, we need to go back again to Europe. As I said before many Jews suffered so much from Christian and nationalist persecutions in Europe, they came to believe that the solution was to get away from religion altogether.

These Socialists believed that the great "equalizer" was to be secular. For them, religion was at the root source of all of Europe's problems. All the wars that were taking place in Europe over the centuries were based on religion and national ethnicity. Socialism/Communism was the system by which everyone was equal, and if the world would only adopt this system, there would finally be peace on Earth, because everyone would be a Socialist. Unify the World through a Globalist Socialist system. Then there would be no more reason for war.

Naturally, to this day, it has not been possible to permanently suppress the various Christian churches in Europe as well as the firmly entrenched ethnic delineations through Socialism/Communism as in the case of Yugoslavia until its breakup in 1990, but there was a period of relative peace between the different ethnic groups under Socialism/ Communism from 1945 to 1990. This was to end with a big bang during the breakup of the Yugoslav Republic.

All the animosities of the centuries were buried under layers of Communist/Socialist "cement" until an "earthquake" brought back all the old ethnic wars between Catholics, Moslems and Orthodox Christians and accounts to be settled.

As for the Jews of Europe, when Theodore Herzl predicted in 1897 that within 50 years there would arise in the Holy Land a Jewish state known as Israel, all these wars of religion, nationalism and Socialism were then transferred by the Jewish people reflecting the countries and belief systems these Jews came from. Now the Jews brought these rival ideologies from Europe to the malarial swamps, bare mountains and deserts of the Holy Land.

Indeed there were many Jews, most Jews, in fact, who refused to consider the Holy Land as the future of the Jewish people. So many remained in Europe, or scattered throughout the rest of the world. And indeed Jews played a central role in the rise of Communism in Russia and later in other East European countries until they were purged and annihilated by the same Communist/Socialist systems the Jews created. Some people estimate that in the course of the purging the Communist party of its Jews, Stalin indeed killed up to one million Jews during his decades of tyranny in addition to

112

the sum odd 40 million Russian and Ukrainian Christians he killed. It was a Communist Holocaust of both Christians and Jews.

Many Jews just opted out and chose the road of assimilation, secularism, disconnection from the Jewish nation, basically disappearing from the history books.

My attention will focus on the Jews of Europe who were basically divided into three groups: Religious, Socialist and nationalist, just like the Europeans Christians. (Of course, there were those who just opted out and assimilated as well, but they remain irrelevant until Hitler rediscovered them and annihilated them including the assimilated and disconnect from Judaism, in the Nazi Holocaust.)

The religious Jews were divided up into many groups, many of which were hostile to each other. There were the Hassidim who were mystical and opposed the "letter of the law." They were considered heretics by the Misnagdim, the textural literalists who controlled Jewish life at that time. Amongst the Hassidim, there were many divisions as well, but most of these groups were anti-Zionist and believed that there could be no moving to a new life in the Holy Land unless the Messiah brought them home to Israel.

Amongst the Socialists/Communists, there were those who believed that Mother Russia was the solution, and yet others who had no faith in the Russian people ever being friendly to the Jews deciding that a Socialist/Communist state in the Holy Land was the only solution for Jewish people.

After WWII, there were kibbutzim (socialist collective settlements) that were torn asunder by internal ideological debate: Was Josef Stalin, dictator of Russia, the true leader of the Jews in Israel or not. Families were torn apart by the debate and many couples divorced over the ideological issue as to whether their first allegiance was to Prime Minister Ben-

Gurion of Israel or to Stalin of the Soviet Union. But there was always a strong ideological affinity to Russia because it was the root of Communism/Socialism.

There used to be a popular joke in Israel: Mother Russia, Father Stalin...Wouldn't it be great if we were orphans?!"

The nationalists all believed in making aliyah (moving) to Israel "one day" as the inevitable destiny of the Jewish people, though many nationalists tarried and remained in Europe until the Nazis reached them and destroyed them because of their inability to escape Europe and to receive "certificates" allowing them into British Mandatory Palestine. And today, there are many who call themselves "Jewish nationalists" but have not yet made it to Israel permanently, but for different reasons, usually financial. Usually moving to Israel involves a financial sacrifice. I should know!

Indeed, there was a great resistance amongst all groups as to the timing of when the Jews should go to Israel to live if at all. There were two assassination attempts on the life of Ze'ev Vladimir Jabotinsky, the founder of Zionist nationalism because he insisted on immediately transferring all the Jews of Europe to the Land of Israel.

After WWI and the pogroms the Petlura in the Ukraine, it was Jabotinsky who in 1920 predicted the Holocaust a generation later. He warned the Jews in Europe: "Liquidate the Diaspora, or the Diaspora will liquidate you!" By the way, it is interesting that the two assassination attempts on Jabotinsky came not from the Socialists but from the ultra-Orthodox Jews in Europe who felt that Jabotinsky was threatening the raisson d'etre of rabbinical leaders and their hierarchies. Europe was seen as the center of civilization. Moving to the "Promised Land" was seen as a wild dream, something that would end life in "civilized" Europe as the Jews knew it. Even my own grandparents who moved to

Argentina in 1924 were criticized by those relatives who remained in Poland for trading off "civilization" in Warsaw to living with the wild Indians in the "Pampas." But Jabotinsky was right, and unfortunately many of these Jews who chose not to leave Europe died in the Holocaust.

Jabotinsky, born in Odessa, Russia in 1880, was a typical 19th century "liberal" European much like Theodore Herzl of Austro-Hungary. He believed in laissez faire capitalism and the superiority of free-minded intellectualism. He was a believer in Judeo-Christian Western Civilization and Democracy. But when he saw the excesses of the pogroms against the Jews in Eastern Europe during his service as an officer in the British Army, and especially the Petlura pogroms in the Ukraine during the Russian Revolution (1917-1920) between the Communist Red Army and the Whites armies which were anti-Communist nationalists, Jabotinsky decided that radical measures were needed first to defend the Jews of Europe and secondly to get them en masse to the Holy Land before an impending Holocaust could take place.

There were many in the Communist/Socialist world who viewed Jabotinsky as a nationalist/fascist because of his radical solution to the Jewish problem in Europe. And as I said in Chapter I of this book, we of the Betar Youth Movement were hated by the Socialists because of our "Blue Shirts" just as Socialists in Europe hated the Brown Shirts in Germany and the Black Shirts in Italy. But we Betarim were never violent and murderous as the Black or Brown shirts. We were just naively romantic and dreamers, whereas the Socialists were "down to Earth" people who controlled everything in Israel.

There were also clearly alliances between the Jabotinsky nationalists and the Fascists of Italy under Mussolini until Italy adopted the German inspired anti-Semitic Racism

Laws. It was the Italian naval school at Savitavecchia which trained Israel's first sailors and merchant fleet captains.

The return of the Jews to the Holy Land took place in many stages. Firstly, the Jews had never totally left the Holy Land from the time of the Roman Empire. There were always Jews in the Holy Land. Throughout the last 2,000 years, there were Jewish people coming home to live in the Holy Land as opposed to those Jews who emigrated seeking better opportunities abroad. But our physical ties to the Land of Israel were always there even though life was extremely hard and dangerous.

In 1867, Mark Twain visited the Holy Land and wrote a book "Innocents Abroad." He described the Holy Land as a barren, miserable country. He traveled two days without seeing a single soul. The countryside was devoid of residents. Most of the Jews lived in Jerusalem, Tiberias or Safed. Mark Twain is quoted as saying: "If this is the Promised Land, I sure don't want it promised to me!"

Jews were already returning to the Land of Israel from Europe in the late 1800's from Russia and Eastern Europe. But there were also Jews who came on foot or on donkey from Afghanistan, Iran, Kurdistan, Yemen as well as other Islamic countries. There was a messianic feeling in the air that the time had come for the Jews to return home.

At the 1st Zionist Congress in Basel, Switzerland in 1897, Theodore Herzl predicted that within 50 years (1947) there would be a Jewish State in Israel. He was right. He was a prophet.

But the fact is that the people who dominated the Zionist movement were Socialists and their religious allies. The nationalists were in the minority. The Jewish Agency or the prototype of the future Israeli governments was controlled by the Socialists.

116

In 1923, there was a complete split between the Socialists and the followers of Jabotinsky who became known as the Revisionists. The religious groups sided with the Socialists who controlled the purse-strings of the Jewish settlement in Israel.

One of the reasons for the split was the British decision in 1922 to sever territories from the Palestine Mandate in order to form the Hashemite Kingdom of Jordan. The Balfour Declaration of 1917 had called for a "Jewish Homeland in Palestine". In 1917 this meant for the Revisionists a Jewish Homeland in all of Palestine meaning from the Mediterranean to Iraq. The British had, in effect, severed 2/3 of the mandate in order to placate the squabbling House of Saud and Hashemite families of Saudi Arabia. In order to make peace in Arabia, the Hashemites were given Jordan, Syria and Iraq. The House of Saud took over Arabia, hence Saudi Arabia.

The Revisionists saw this as a betrayal, the first of many, by the British. Now the Jews were left with only 1/3 of the original promise of the British for a Jewish Homeland.

I think it is fair to say that the Revisionists have always been seen as maximalists and the Socialists as minimalists when it comes to territory. It was also in 1922 that Mussolini rose to power in Italy, and the Jewish Revisionists who had an affinity to the Fascists of Mussolini became hated and expelled by the Socialists everywhere possible. It was in the 1920's that Mussolini started his conquests in Libya, Somalia, and Ethiopia.

The Socialists were now ensconced in power and controlled the Jewish leadership in the Land of Israel from Day #1. The Revisionists were "outside of the game." But because there were many Jews in Europe and especially in Poland and the Baltic states who were anti-Socialist because of the nationalist governments in those countries and especially Pilsudski in Poland, the Betarim and Revisionists received sufficient support to survive, even if persecuted by the Socialist establishment in Israel. There was also support from Jews in America and the West.

Most or these "rightwing" Betarim and Revisionists were middle class people who found employment in the private market as lawyers, doctors, professionals and businessmen.

The greatness of the Socialists was in a system that was brutal on its own people. These socialists, who did not believe in God, came home to Israel to find malarial swamps, bare mountains and deserts. Over two millennia, the Holy Land was neglected by wave after wave of pillaging invaders: Romans, Byzantines, Persians, Arabs, Crusaders, and finally Turks. The land was ravaged and denuded of its trees especially by the Turks.

The Ottoman Turks had a law placing a tax on all non-fruit-bearing trees as a sign of the landowner's wealth. So landowners would cut down the non-fruit-bearing trees to avoid paying that tax. Later on as the Turks built their railroads in the Holy Land, trees were chopped down to provide wood for burning in the locomotives as well as the laying of railroad ties.

As the trees were all chopped down (except for fruit bearing orchards), the top soil would have nothing to hold on it, since the roots would die soon after the tree was gone. Thus the topsoil washed into the valleys creating malarial swamps. There was the Negev desert in the south of the country as well as many parts of the Mediterranean coast which were sand dunes.

The socialist idealists started returning home and forming collective settlements. They did not believe in God, but they did believe in what the labor of their hands could create:

a Garden of Eden paradise in the Land of Israel, all under Socialism.

These people underwent terrible suffering as they broke the stones with their bare hands, planted trees, drained the swamps and planted the crops. Indeed, when the Zionist movement in Europe began purchasing land from absentee Arab landlords who preferred to live in Beirut or Damascus, the absentee landlords, also known as effendis readily sold their land to these "crazy" Jews knowing that the land would revert back to them when the Jews all died of Malaria and other diseases, gave up and fled the Holy Land.

But these pioneers did not give up. They did succeed in healing the Holy Land of 2,000 years of neglect and barrenness. It was when the effendis realized that the Jews were succeeding and staying on the land, and that the land would not revert to the effendis because the Jews had converted many areas into lush gardens, that it was then decided to start fighting the Jews because otherwise, the land would indeed become a homeland for the Jews, and this was contrary to Islam.

There were riots in 1920, 1921, 1927, 1929, the Arab revolt from 1936-39 and finally the Naqba or "disaster" of the Arabs commonly known as Israel's Independence in 1948.

The Socialist ideology was "dunam po, dunam sham," which means an acre here and an acre there. The Socialist Zionist approach to conquering the land was the legal purchase, parcel by parcel, of any lot of land put up for sale by the Arabs and the settlement of Jews in a determined organized manner. It was an evolutionary system compared to the "revolutionary" system of the Revisionists.

The Jabotinsky/Revisionist approach was to take 500,000 Polish Jewish Betar members, put them on Italian warships and invade Palestine, kick out the British administration and create a Jewish State by force. This was not considered reality by the Socialists who were seen as "underachievers" by the frustrated nationalists.

The Socialists saw the Revisionists as dreamers and romantics.

It was the socialist pioneers who converted the land from a hell to a lush garden, Socialist though it may be. At the same time, there were Revisionists who privately bought land from the Arabs, settled in Israel and planted their own gardens as well. But it was primarily the Socialists who did the planting of trees and the paving of roads where there was complete wilderness.

But the Yishuv, or Jewish settlement of the Palestine Mandate was facing a number of problems. One was the colonial "White Papers" of the British Foreign Office. On the one hand, the British had rewarded the Jews for their loyalty during WWI by creating a "homeland" in Palestine. But immediately after this, the pressures from the Arabs to stop Jewish immigration mounted. The British succumbed to this and began limiting Jewish immigration to Palestine on an increasing scale.

Secondly, it was the rise of Hitler in Germany that brought about a direct existential threat to millions of Jews in Europe. Jabotinsky's prophecy: "Liquidate the Diaspora or the Diaspora will liquidate you" was becoming a self-fulfilling prophecy. Now more and more Jews were seeking a mass exodus from Europe. The British closed the gates tighter and tighter.

The British allowed only a very few Jews into Palestine. "Certificates" were issued to the Jewish Agency by the British Colonial Office, and the Jewish Agency of course gave preferential treatment to their own kind i.e. the Socialists of

Europe. The nationalists and religious Jews of Europe were not seen as the element the new homeland needed to drain swamps and plant crops in the collectivized settlements.

So the nationalists and the religious were trapped in Europe.

At the same time in 1936-39, during the Arab Revolt, the British and the Jews had to deal with a full-fledged military campaign with the Arabs who wanted both the Jews and the British out of the land.

It was an extreme situation and the Jewish nationalists chose an extreme solution: fighting the British in order to expel them from Palestine and replace the Palestine Mandate with the Jewish State of Israel. Again, the "minimalist" approach of the Socialists was to cooperate with British even if it meant sacrificing the Jews of Europe. The Socialist idea was "a kibbutz here and kibbutz there." Every advance under the noses of the British would strengthen the Jewish Yishuv in Palestine. The Socialists felt that confrontation with the British would be counter-productive.

The Socialists were right, but the nationalists for their part were also right. If the Arab plan was to kill the Jews, to have the British "lock" in the Jews into Nazi Europe, and then leave it to Hitler to finish off the Jews, how could the Jews sit back with only "a kibbutz here and kibbutz there?" Radical action had to be taken otherwise the British would never leave the Palestine Mandate as their central military base in the Middle East.

The Socialists created the Hagannah (in Hebrew "The Defense") and the nationalist/Revisionists created the Irgun Tzvai Leumi (in Hebrew "The National Military Organization). It was mostly the Hagannah troops which volunteered to serve in the British military as the Palestine Brigade in WWII while most of the Irgun people fought

121

the British. In 1942, there was a temporary truce between the Irgun and Hagannah and the British and it was decided that both Jewish underground military forces would join the British army to fight the Nazis who were dangerously close to conquering Palestine in 1942. A splinter group of the Irgun rejecting the truce with the Hagannah broke away calling itself the Lehi or Lohamei Herut Israel (in Hebrew: "Fighters for the Freedom of Israel").

By the way, it was David Raziel of the Irgun who was killed in Iraq fighting for the British against the Nazis, and it was Moshe Dayan of the Hagannah who lost an eye in Syria fighting for the British against the pro-Nazi Vichy French. Thousands of Palestinians (Jews) died fighting for the allies against the Nazis. The Moslems fought alongside the Nazis and the SS.

With the end of WWII, the dimensions of the Holocaust catastrophe became known. Six million Jews were dead and one million survivors wanted to leave Europe to come home to Israel. But the British continued with their White Papers blocking all except just a few from coming home. Now the Cold War between Communism and the West was causing the British to continue pandering to the Arabs so as to prevent them from going over to the Communists. (During WWII, the fear was that the Arabs would go over to the Nazis. But it is always the Jews who are sacrificed "for the good of the cause.")

Again, it was the maximalists vs. the minimalists. The Socialists tried passive non-violent resistance and illegal smuggling into the country of immigrants. The famous movie "Exodus" based on the novel by Leon Uris is a taste of what it was like at that time. The Irgun and Lehi maximalists started an open rebellion against the British attacking their soldiers and installations in Palestine.

It must also be remembered that the British had envisioned Palestine as its land-based "aircraft carrier" in the Middle East. The British wanted to keep Palestine as its colony in perpetuity. After six million Jews were killed in Europe and one million refugees remained in internment camps in Europe, all the attentions of the Jewish people were now focused on getting rid of the British, the Socialists by non-violent means the nationalists by terrorism and warfare.

With the blowing up by the Irgun of the King David Hotel in 1947 which served as a headquarters for the British military, it was decided by the Socialist leadership and the Hagannah to clamp down on the nationalists because the latter were perceived by the Socialists as threatening the entire settlement project of the Jews in Palestine.

An "Open Season" was declared. Hagannah members and Socialists would hunt down nationalists and hand them over to the British for jailing, expulsion to other countries, and execution. Very often, brute violence was employed to beat up Irgun members in the streets, and Socialists ended up killing a few and injuring many. Ariel Sharon was one of these Hagannah members who participated in this hunt for right-wing people. Socialists Jews were persecuting and betraying fellow Jews in order to save the Socialist Zionist project. Many nationalists were fired from their jobs because of their rightwing beliefs. The Irgun people did not fight back because it did not believe that a Jew should ever raise his hand against a fellow Jew, not like the Socialists for whom violence against fellow Jews was acceptable. Again it was the Russian Communist tradition to purge anyone who did not toe the official line with whatever force and violence was deemed necessary, all, of course, "for the good of the cause."

In April of 1948, a month before Israel's independence an

123

Irgun gun-running ship, the Altalena approached the shores of Tel-Aviv with a load of weapons for the Irgun. It was reputed to be carrying enough weapons for the Irgun to liberate Jerusalem. David Ben-Gurion, head of the Jewish Agency at that time and a month later, Israel's first prime minister sought a Hagannah officer who would give the orders to sink the ship and murder the young sailors on board. Famous Israeli officers such as Yigal Allon and Yigal Yadin refused to carry out the orders. Yitzhak Rabin was the third candidate. He agreed to give the orders to his men, and the ship was sunk. Ben-Gurion wanted to deny the Irgun these weapons because he saw the Irgun as a rival. The back of the Irgun had to be broken in order to assure the Hagannah's absolute control, and it was the sinking of the Altalena which did it. Sixteen defenseless sailors were murdered by Rabin's men as they swam to the shore. They were not shooting at anyone. They were just swimming to shore and were murdered on orders by Yitzhak Rabin. Menahem Begin, head of the Irgun, and later to be prime minister of Israel in 1977, gave orders to the Irgun not to respond to this provocation, thereby preventing a fratricidal civil war in Israel. The approach of the Irgun and the Revisionist/Nationalists has always been to refrain from internecine conflict. Jew must never lift up his hand against fellow Jew. We must always be benevolent to our brothers even if they swing an axe at us.

A month later, Israel declared its independence on May 15th, 1948. The population of Israel was 648,000 at that time, and six million Jewish people were dead in Europe. A million survivors now wanted to come home to Israel from the killing fields of Europe, and about another one million Jews were expelled from Arab/Islamic countries. Within two years Israel's population grew by two million to about 2 1/2 million people from 648,000 Jews in 1948.

124

Again it is not the purpose of this humble book to even try to tell Israel's story from the date of Israel's birth. But it is important to show the trends of political thinking of the Jews of Israel and much of this depends on understanding the ethnic backgrounds of those who came to live in this Land of Israel.

It is fair to say that an overwhelming majority of Israel's 648,000 Jewish people in 1948 was pro-Socialist. These were the people who were allowed in by the British and the Socialist leadership of the Yishuv. Nationalists and religious received very few of the British "certificates" to enter the Palestine Mandate. Now, all of a sudden in 1948, the gates swing wide open and two million people are added to the "established" Jews.

Now, no longer were the Socialists the overwhelming majority but were basically outnumbered by very bitter people: Jews who survived the Holocaust in Europe, many of whom were religious or nationalists, or Jews from Moslem countries for whom the Socialism of Eastern Europe transplanted to Israel was a foreign system.

The Socialists now had a challenge to face. They had to indoctrinate as many of these newcomers as possible, "convert" them into Socialists or eventually face the loss of power.

The "carrot and the stick" were very successful from 1948 until 1977 to ensure that the Labor Party (i.e. the Socialists) would remain pre-eminent in the Israeli political scene. One could not get a job in the "administration" or "establishment" unless one obtained a red membership card in the Histadrut, which to this day is the Labor Party's way of controlling Israel's economy. The Histadrut is Israel's equivalent to America's AFL-CIO labor union, plus being a sick fund, plus being a pension fund. No red booklet of membership, no employment.

The nationalists had to rely on one another to get jobs or go into private business, or emigrate abroad.

Financial aid poured into Israel from all over the Jewish world. There was also some aid coming from the United States. Israel Bonds was an investment program to encourage Jews as well as non-Jews to invest in Israel with interest paid scrupulously on time. Israel became an economic miracle, but the economy was controlled very much by the Labor Party. They controlled the government. They directed where these monies from abroad were being invested and spent.

Again if one was not of the Labor Party, one needed to look for employment with people of a like mindset. And if one could not find employment, one eventually had to leave Israel. According to Sergio de la Pergola, Israel's foremost statistician, about three million Jews left Israel since 1948, mostly for lack of employment possibilities.

It must be remembered that in almost all small countries, the infrastructure will always be too small and truncated to provide employment as the Western countries of Europe or the America's could provide.

Again there are those of maximalist and minimalist approaches. Israel survived and grew under the Labor Party's tutelage from 1948 to 1977, until it was replaced by the rightwing Likud Party for the first time, because the people had had enough Socialism.

From 1952 until the eve of the Six Day War on June 5, 1967, Israel's population grew to about three million and remained fixed at that number. Israel went into an economic depression known in Hebrew as Mitun. Many people started leaving the country, more than the usual.

After the Six Day War and until 1973, Israel's population grew to about 3.5 million thanks mainly to immigration from the Soviet Union. But these immigrants were mostly anti-Socialist and anti-Communist coming out of the Soviet Union. The tide was turning against the Socialist founders of Israel. By 1977, four years later, Labor lost its control of the government for the first time because the majority of the population was now rightwing and anti-Socialist.

But Menahem Begin, Israel's first prime minister from the rightwing Likud Party continued the tradition of Jews not raising their hands against fellow Jews. So he decided not to confront the Labor controlled labor unions and civil service but attempted to work with the established Civil Service. There was none of this Stalinist control that had existed until 1977. There were no firing squads. There were no purges as had regularly taken place in the Soviet Union. The rightwing Likud was now the governing party, but reconciliation between Right and Left was the name of the game.

So the Labor Party continued to silently rule Israel even though the party now leading Israel's political coalition was not the Labor Party. It is true that many rightwing activists could now seek employment in the civil service and government, but after a few years, very often, the Labor Party stalwarts who were always in power from day #1, eventually found ways to weed out these rightwing people and purge them from the ranks of the civil service.

One of the central experiences of my life as a civil servant occurred during the period 1989-90 in the Government Press Office, part of the prime minister's office under Yitzhak Shamir.

I had been employed as a senior editor and translator in the News Department of the GPO and worked for one year very closely with Yoram Ettinger who was Director of the GPO. I got my job without any "proteksia" or insiders pulling strings. I worked seven and a half hours a day for six days a

127

week for a salary of only about $500 a month. My specialty was translating Israeli military intelligence coverage of the Islamic and Arabic press from Hebrew to English for the foreign press. (Israeli Military Intelligence would translate from Arabic and Persian into Hebrew, and my job was to retranslate these news articles into English.)

When Yoram Ettinger was chosen by Prime Minister Yitzhak to serve in Israel's Embassy in Washington, DC, as liaison to the conservative and Christian members of Congress, I continued to work under my new boss who at first was friendly and recommended me for promotion. After six months under the new boss, I applied for and won a tender for my position. The winning of the tender entitled me after six more months to receive job security or tenure. Theoretically, I could not be fired now. I needed this tenure in order to secure a mortgage in order to buy an apartment to replace the home we lost as a result of the failed Waterpik business. I was now forty years old and need the "job security" and should have gotten it.

After two years at my job, working myself to the bone, and harming my eyesight in front of the computer for seemingly endless hours, I decided to approach my civil servant superiors to ask when I would receive my tenure, as promised by the law. "Law? What law? Go to the law. And besides, we know your political views."

I was fired by these Socialist bureaucrats, and lies and stupid remarks were put in file which I will not bore the readers with. When I demanded an internal enquiry in the Prime Minister's Office, I was vindicated by Director-General Yossi Ben-Aharon and my first boss Yoram Ettinger. Ben-Aharon asked me what I wanted now. I said, "I want my job back."

He answered: "No, you don't. They are waiting for you.

128

They will make you sick. They are waiting for you. They will kill you in that office. Can't you do better than $500 a month elsewhere?"

I answered him, "But I am old (41). What kind of job can I get in the Israeli government? I am a marked man."

He answered: "After 40, you are finished with the diapers. Now go and serve God."

And that's what I did! And that's one of the reasons I am writing this book!

I was fired from the prime minister's office by Socialist Labor Party members in October 1990 and a month later, I was in Texas starting my new life speaking in churches, synagogues, radio and TV. This new work replaced the old slavery of burning my eyes out in front of the computer with zero appreciation for my services. I have now spoken in over 400 churches and 40 synagogues around the world in the US, Canada and Europe. These people in the Government Press Office did me a favor, though I did not think it to be a favor then.

Continuing with the expose, from a military perspective, it is true that the Israel Defense Forces formed out of the Hagannah, Irgun and Lehi groups fought valiantly and successfully to stave off Arab invasions and attacks. But the IDF's officer cadres were primarily drawn from the Socialist Hagannah and Palmach elite troops. Soldiers and officers from the Irgun and Lehi, were always relegated to secondary commands and were never promoted to top positions in the IDF. And even though officers like Ezer Weizman and Ariel Sharon became members of the rightwing Likud that is not how they started. They all started as Socialists (and returned to their roots later in life.)

Again, in my own humble capacity of author of this book, I have another example of how Socialism dealt with people like me in my military service.

My military record is hardly anything out of the ordinary. As an immigrant, I served in my compulsory service for one year as member of the Judea-Samaria Command Spokesman's Office under Lt. Col. Raphael Horowitz. I was a "Mamak" or academic rank officer who spent most of my time processing Palestinians who were coming to live in the Judea, Samaria and Gaza areas under the "Family Reunification" program. I was basically an immigration and naturalization bureaucrat.

I was released in January 1973 with the shortened service period done by married immigrants and was then remobilized as an artillery crewman during the Yom Kippur War which began on October 5th, 1973. I served 17 years in this same unit with the same artillery crew. Now I was just a private greasing howitzers and carrying 94 lbs artillery shells. I was the #4, the man who pulled the lanyard thus firing the cannon.

In 1989, our howitzers were changed requiring only six crew members instead of 12. Since I was over the age of 40, it was decided to transfer me and the rest of the "old guys" either to Civil Defense or the IDF Spokesman. Again, I was recommended by Lt. Col. Horowitz to return to the IDF Spokesman's Office in Tel Aviv. In 1993, I underwent officer/spokesman's training and served in this unit as a lieutenant for 13 years. In 1993, I volunteered to serve more than 90 days in the reserves, kind of a record for peacetime. In total, I served thirty years in the IDF reserves and was "retired" with a certificate thanking me for doing my share. (Most Israeli males do not serve thirty years in the reserves!)

My immediate commander was a wonderful lady by the name of Irit Atzmon. Lt. Col. Irit Atzmon was in charge of public relations. She served with distinction and was very friendly toward me, personally. She even tried to arrange a job for me when officer slots became available. I never did get the positions, but I don't fault her for this. Very good men, all of them known to me got these positions by their own merits. I suppose God wanted me not to get those positions but to continue my work in the churches and synagogues abroad, primarily in the US.

Toward the end of the summer of 1995, Rabbi Norman Singer of the Ohev Sholom Synagogue in Williamsport, Pennsylvania died suddenly of a heart attack. It was two weeks before the Jewish High Holy Days. Since my best friend, Clifford Rieders was president of the synagogue, he earnestly requested that I fill in, or "pinch-hit" as rabbi until a new rabbi could be found. I was not a rabbi but had just completed the MA program at Israel's branch of the Jewish Theological Seminary in Jerusalem. Cliff said, "We will never find a rabbi to fill Singer's position two weeks before Rosh Hashanah."

So I was hired for a total of 70 days to fill in as congregational rabbi, 30 days for the period of the High Holy Days and 40 days more until December 1st and a new rabbi was chosen.

As part of my job, I was to provide an adult education class once a week. Since I was fresh out of seminary, I had plenty of material and enjoyed doing this.

One day, I received a call from someone by the name of Ernst Bloch, leader of a group called "Pro-Israel." He asked me if I was rabbi, and I said, "Yes, temporarily." The purpose of his call was to offer for free a lecturer on the topic of the controversial Oslo Agreements between Israel and the Palestinians. I thought I could incorporate this lecture as part of the adult education program in the synagogue.

Bloch was offering me a lecturer by the name of Moshe Leshem, a former colonel in Israel's Defense Forces who had crossed the Suez Canal in 1973 with Ariel Sharon in the brilliant counterattack which turned Israel's near defeat into a stunning military victory and almost wiped out Egypt's military in the winter of 1974.

Leshem was critical of the Oslo Accords and was convinced they threatened Israel's existence. Bloch was ready to pay for airline tickets for Leshem to come to Williamsport, Pennsylvania to address my synagogue for free. All I had to do was to say, "Yes."

I consulted with Cliff Rieders, synagogue president, and he agreed. Cliff told me that the Israeli Consulate in Philadelphia was always sending pro-Oslo Accord speakers and it would be refreshing for a change to have someone opposed to the accords, someone with another viewpoint.

But in all fairness, as rabbi, and as an Israeli Army Spokesman in the reserves, I decided to call the Israeli consulate in Philadelphia to ask for a pro-Oslo spokesman two weeks after Leshem was to speak to be "balanced." All of this was done with the approval of the synagogue board. (It must be emphasized at this point that I was not to tell the Israeli Consulate in Philadelphia that we were hosting Leshem, two weeks before their spokesman arrived because then the synagogue would be put on a "black list" as a "right-wing" synagogue and no spokesman would be sent. Jews in America who had even a hint of being right-wing were blacklisted by the Israeli consulates and embassies globally during the Rabin Administration. There was zero toleration of any view other than that of the Left, much in the tradition of Soviet Communism and Socialism.) As an IDF spokesman, I was trained not to delve into politics but to be balanced and share the IDF approach to political accords. (I spoke about this previously in Chapter V when I spoke about Globalism.)

132

As an IDF Spokesman, I made it clear to the members of the synagogue that there were indeed pros and cons to the debate about Israel ceding territories to the Palestinians. Both sides of the issue had to be aired. Everyone unanimously agreed.

Now, I wanted to add that I was no newcomer to the synagogue. I had spoken many times in the synagogue as an IDF spokesman and scholar in residence.

Interestingly, at times, I would return to Israel on my breaks between lecture circuits abroad and report for duty at the IDF Spokesman's Office. I always coordinated my home visits with the IDF Spokesman's office in order to serve my yearly quota of reserves duty. On occasion, Lt. Col. Irit Atzmon would say to me that she was receiving complaints from the United States about my message. It turns out that an Israeli young lady and her parents who lived in Williamsport, Pennsylvania, in whom I had placed my trust and who knew Lt. Col. Atzmon were calling her long distance to denounce me for "my rightwing views." You see, they were Socialists/Communists from Romania who had lived some years in Israel and now left Israel to seek their livelihoods in the US. But when it came to fulfilling their "Socialist obligations" of slandering right-wingers, they made sure to call Israel in the true traditions of Communists and Socialists to denounce me to Irit Atzmon, who after all, was also a member of the Socialist elite that has always controled Israel's military.

But getting back to Moshe Leshem, he was to arrive on Tuesday, November 7th, 1995 to address the congregation. On Saturday, November 4th, Yitzhak Rabin was assassinated, and now a decision had to be made by myself and the synagogue leadership as to whether we should cancel Leshem's visit or not. It was decided that on the contrary, it is more important now than ever to discuss all aspects of the peace process. But at the same time, we should turn the evening into a memorial for Yitzhak Rabin. And indeed, as rabbi, I conducted what many people considered a beautiful memorial service for Rabin. I placed advertisements in the local press inviting even the non-Jews of Williamsport to attend. The synagogue was packed, and we paid homage to Rabin in addition to hearing "another opinion" on the Oslo Accords.

Moshe Leshem provided an in depth analysis of the Oslo Accords. He explained how there was no way any member of the Israel Knesset could have even read it with the short time available before the signing. Leshem's only fault was that he was one-sided and would not consent to the fact that there were also pros to the Oslo Accords. Members of the synagogue asked, "If the agreement is so bad, how could someone as famous as Rabin agree to it?" He answered: "I don't know."

So I took up the cudgels on behalf of the leftwing pro-Oslo leadership of Israel, and explained the Israeli Army position that missiles did not stop at borders, and therefore, peace was the left's approach on how better to maintain Israel's security because with peace no unstoppable missiles with nuclear warheads would be fired. I considered myself very loyal to my position as rabbi and IDF Spokesman's Office. I have always believed in being objective and giving both sides of the story.

Toward the end of the evening, the Romanian Socialist parents of the lady who had served under Irit Atzmon and who had been calling her to denounce me over a period of years entered the meeting at the synagogue and started to disrupt the proceedings. They pointed their fingers at me and at Leshem and said: "You rightwing people are all guilty of Rabin's murder." They then walked out of the meeting. They had not heard me defending Rabin's rationale for supporting the Oslo Accords.

Two days later, Thursday, November 9th, at about 5 in the morning, my phone rings in Williamsport, Pennsylvania. It was Lt. Col Irit Atzmon calling me long distance from Tel Aviv with a speaker phone to court martial me in the presence of the IDF General Staff for being part of the group that murdered Rabin. The spirit in Israel after Rabin's assassination is that all right-wingers were murderers of Rabin.

After I explained my "defense" to Atzmon, I faxed newspaper articles and advertisements about the memorial service I had conducted in memory of Yitzhak Rabin and even phone bills to the Israeli Consulate to prove that I had invited a pro-Oslo speaker from the Israeli government. I was vindicated in the telephone court-martial but I never received the rank of captain in the reserves as I should have. This was the same spirit of the Altalena and the Open Season against members of the Irgun that was resurfacing in 1995 forty years later. Now I was the victim. Nothing had changed it seems, from the 1940's. Now I was experiencing this on my own skin 6,000 miles away from Israel.

I told Irit Atzmon: "Here I am in the US, in Williamsport, Pennsylvania, trying to make a living as rabbi of a synagogue because I cannot get a job in Israel. I am away from Israel eight months of the year doing what I believe is a service to Israel and Jewish People. Have you all gone mad in the IDF and Israeli Civil Service?"

Similarly, Israel's Civil Service was manned by hand chosen people of the Labor Party. Right-wing nationalists had better look for employment in the private market.

By the way, there is a joke that typifies the nepotism of the early period in Israel:

"Israel's first Prime Minister David Ben-Gurion was

135

looking for someone to fill the critically important position of prime minister's financial adviser.

So the Israeli Civil Service issued a tender for the position after duly publicizing this in Israel's newspapers. Over a thousand people applied. After incredibly difficult tests and screening, three candidates remained. At the final interview to decide who got the job, they were asked: "How much is five and five?"

The first candidate answered: "Eleven". The second candidate answered: "Nine". The Third candidate answered: "Ten."

Who got the job? Ben-Gurion's nephew got the job. This joke is based on the nepotism shown in Israel's civil service.

Again, if one is a new immigrant and is seeking to attain employment, buy an apartment or home, feed his family and cannot get a job, he or she will eventually have to leave Israel. And if you have so many people fighting over very few positions available, it is clear many people will leave the country. I should know. I am a perfect example of this.

At this point, I would like to return to what I consider relevant details in the growth of Israel's population from 1973. The country stagnated demographically from 1973 until 1989 and the population remained at 3.5 million Jews. Again, envision a family size Coca Cola bottle pouring its contents into a small Coca Cola bottle. Once the little bottle is full, no matter how much more you pour into it, it will overflow and the contents are lost. This is the case in Israel, which is the little Coca Cola bottle. The family size bottle is the Diaspora and the lost contents are the Jews who cannot find jobs in Israel. They are eventually lost or return to the family size bottle overseas.

At this point, I want to relate some more about my

personal experiences in Israel. From 1968 to 1971, I studied at Hebrew University in Jerusalem to complete my BA in Sovietology and Latin American and Spanish Studies. From 1972-3 I served in my compulsory military service. From 1974-6 I worked as a salaried employee in import-export firms in Jerusalem. From 1976 to 1986 I worked as Teledyne Waterpik's exclusive agent for Israel operating a store in Clal Center in Jerusalem and another store in Dizengoff Center in Tel-Aviv.

There were many reasons for my discontinuing this work, but I suppose it is fair for people who believe in God to say, "It was not God's will or my destiny to continue importing Waterpiks to Israel."

In 1987, I worked for a year as a real estate agent, and in 1988 I was hired by the Likud Party under Dr. Eliahu Ben-Elissar to help edit and translate the Likud Election Campaign Plank in Hebrew and into English and Spanish.

It was after my bitter experiences in business in Israel that I began to understand how difficult it was to make a living as a businessman in Israel. I was now 38 years old, without a job and seeing Israel as a country whose population was stunted from 1973 to 1989.

Since I was now looking toward the world of Israeli politics to continue to fulfill my destiny, I was trying to understand what was wrong in Israel and how to fix it.

I devised a plan, which I will discuss in Chapter VII about attracting investments to Israel and breaking the bottleneck that was frustrating Israel's population growth. But the Israeli politicians, all of whom I knew from university days, were not interested in my positivistic, utopian plans. But I believed then, and I believe now, that I have the answer, and that this economic plan can solve all of Israel's unemployment problems, thus allowing Israel's population to grow.

But it was indeed in 1989 that God intervened by shaking the tree of the Soviet Union. Communism collapsed and all of a sudden there was a deluge of one million immigrants coming to live in Israel. With or without my plans for solving Israel's economic problems, God broke the bottleneck of Israel's truncated economy to ram down our throats one million immigrants. The stagnation caused by Socialism and the failure of Israel's leaders to attract new investments was now overcome by God bringing home all these people first and investments later. So by 1992 Israel's Jewish population grew to almost five million Jews where it has remained for nearly 14 years, again stagnation, again bottlenecks. Jews keep coming to live in Israel, but at the same time, many immigrants and Israelis pick up and leave for lack of work opportunities.

The Likud had come to power in 1977 under Menahem Begin, followed by his successor, Yitzhak Shamir in 1982 after Operation Peace in Galilee (the Lebanon War of 1982). Yoram Aridor, who was then finance minister, instituted a disastrous economic policy encouraging imports and deleting Israel's foreign currency reserves. By 1984, inflation in Israel had reached 383% annually and many businesses were wiped out including my own.

In 1985, a national unity government was formed in which Shimon Peres became prime minister for the first two years to be followed by Yitzhak Shamir for the last two years in a rotation process. By 1988, due to the constant tensions between Peres and Shamir, (the former constantly undercutting the latter), new elections were called. Again, these were the elections I had participated in as assistant to MK Ben-Elissar. With the Likud victory, Shamir was now prime minister until 1992.

As editor of the Likud Election Campaign Plank in 1988,

138

I remember clearly that the Likud called for the following:

1. No withdrawal from the Golan Heights.
2. No negotiations with the PLO.
3. No dealings with Arafat.
4. No Palestinian State.
5. No division of Jerusalem.
6. No withdrawal from the Jordan River as Israel's Eastern security border.

In 1992, the elections were now between Yitzhak Shamir and Yitzhak Rabin. I was shocked to see the Labor Party's campaign plank:

1. No withdrawal from the Golan Heights
2. No negotiations with the PLO.
3. No dealings with Arafat.
4. No Palestinian State.
5. No division of Jerusalem.
6. No withdrawal from the Jordan River as Israel's Eastern security border.

Yitzhak Rabin was portrayed as "Father Security." In polls carried out by the media in 1992, 60% of the Israeli Jews were in favor of some territorial withdrawal for peace but 68% opposed a total return to the borders of 1967. Rabin's campaign plank was "stolen" from the Likud. It was Rabin's ticket to victory.

Again, it has to be emphasized that these million Russians who "came home" to Israel were virulently anti-Communist and pro-rightwing. The Labor Socialists were losing control to the rightwing nationalists and religious parties, so Rabin's strategy was to move to the center in an attempt to steal votes

139

away from Shamir. And he succeeded.

The results of the elections gave Rabin and Labor more votes than Shamir and the Likud. Rabin now had a total of 58 members of Knesset out of a total of 120. But he did not yet have the majority he needed of 61 to form a coalition government.

What did Rabin do? He bribed three MK's from Rafael Eitan's new party Tsomet with Mitsubishi cars and ministerial positions, something patently illegal, and now formed his government. By the way, one of these former ministers, Gonen Segev is now in jail for attempting to smuggle Ecstasy pills into Israel. Here already is an example in 1992 of the corruption institutionalized by Ariel Sharon so threatening Israel today.

The moment Rabin had his 61 member coalition he sprung the Oslo Accords on the people of Israel, an accord which was negotiated secretly and in contravention of Israel's law not to have any contact with the PLO.

Rabin and Labor lied to the people of Israel and broke all six of the promises made in the above points I mentioned. Labor directly copied the Likud's election campaign plank to steal votes from the Likud and then lied to the people by breaking everyone of those promises. And because the Socialist elites controlled Israel's Foreign Ministry, Civil Service and Military, there was nothing the majority of Israelis could do to stop the madness of the Oslo Accords. And the media justified the government. The anger was welling up within the soul of the Israeli people. Rabin was assassinated on November 7th, 1995.

Elections were held in May 1996. Benjamin Netanyahu emerged with a crushing defeat of former Prime Minister Shimon Peres. If the Israeli public was in such mourning for Rabin and if it was so angry at the right-wingers, all of whom

140

murdered Rabin, why did the Likud and rightwing parties win the elections? The reason is that 70% of the Jewish Israelis felt betrayed by what many considered the treason of the left. There was also this anger of how the leftist elites controlled the government, media and much of the business sector.

And at the same time, whenever the Likud and the rightwing was in power, the Socialists leftists, the Labor Party and the Histadrut Labor union would work to subvert and undermine the government, elected by the will of the majority of the Jewish people. In response to the Likud policy to privatize the economy of Israel in order to encourage investments and move away from bankrupt, retarded Socialist practices, the Socialist Histadrut would call strikes that cost the Israeli people billions of dollars and scared away investors. Israel just could not escape the impression it gave the world of being some backwater, corrupt, Ottoman Turkish, Soviet Socialist state which made no sense economically. As a former businessman who lost my business, my home, my car and all my worldly belongings because of this backward system and truncated economy, I think I have a right to express my opinions based on my 38 years in Israel. I have plenty of first-hand experience.

As a result of the constant harassment of Netanyahu and strikes from the leftwing controlled side of Israel's political spectrum, Ehud Barak of Labor succeeded in becoming elected prime minister of Israel in 1999. Also many people on the right-wing abandoned Netanyahu because of the Hebron agreements of 1997 which handed over 80% of the city of Hebron to the Palestinian Authority under terrible pressure from President Bill Clinton. The media and Socialists did a number on Netanyahu, and he temporarily retired from politics after losing the elections.

Netanyahu, for his part, also seemed to behave in a brash, arrogant manner, much in military tradition, thus alienating much of his Likud Party power base. Many branches of the party closed down, and were not reopened until "Papa Bear" Ariel Sharon took control of the Likud. Netanyahu did leave scorched earth within the Likud Party at that time. Many right-wing Jews could not forgive Netanyahu. The Likud lost many votes it would normally have gotten from the right-wingers.

The strategy of newly elected Prime Minister Ehud Barak was the "brilliant idea" of giving away everything or almost everything the Palestinians could possibly want for a peace accord as part of the Camp David II agreements brokered by US President Bill Clinton in June 2000. Even Jerusalem was to be divided in two. The Jewish population was flabbergasted. Barak was seeking a short-cut final agreement with Arafat because the agreement in stages system failed so miserably. The Palestinians were simply not keeping their word.

What was Arafat's response? Intifada II in September 2000. An uprising instigated by Arafat began which killed thousands of Jews and Arabs. This totally unnecessary war started because Arafat was in a predicament. He now had no excuse not to make peace with Israel. The whole world was applying pressure on Arafat to make peace. But if he had agreed then and there at Camp David II in June 2000 to make peace, he was as good as dead, because no Moslem leader can really make peace, real peace with Israel and stay alive. What Ehud Barak really wanted was real peace. Now that Israel was calling Arafat's bluff, Arafat had to respond with a war so terrible that of course, Israel would be blamed for. And it was.

At this point, I want to share another economic anecdote

142

from my Israeli Army Spokesman's Course as well as from my experience as a businessman with contacts in the Palestinian business world.

My Waterpik business had two markets, the Israeli/Jewish market as well as the Palestinian market in Judea, Samaria and Gaza. My Egyptian born wife was very popular wherever we went and we were treated like royalty. We did a good business with the Palestinian Arabs and never had a problem with them. We got to know them. They always kept their word, worked very hard and had the potential of building an economy that theoretically could lead to an economically successful Palestinian autonomy if not state. Some of them had made millions in Saudi Arabia or in South America and even had passports from those countries for having contributed to the economies of those countries. These people, if left alone by the political leaders could work miracles in creating a Palestinian economy. This was my personal experience with these industrialists and entrepreneurs.

From my IDF Spokesman's course in November 1993, just after the signing of the Oslo Agreements on September 13th, 1993, one of our commanders gave us a briefing as to why there would never be a Palestinian State.

He said that to have a state of any kind, you had to give the people bread and butter before you gave them bullets and guns. But Arafat knew nothing of this. He only understood bullets and guns. He never thought of the good of the Palestinian people. He never thought of their welfare.

In order to give the people bread and butter, the businessmen had to succeed in establishing an economic infrastructure for the people to make a living, and hence have bread and butter (sound familiar?). Since Arafat was receiving all these billions of dollars from the US, Europe, and the UN, he theoretically should have been providing much or most of these monies to the businessmen in order for them to succeed in developing an infrastructure for the nascent Palestinian state. But Arafat could not give these businessmen the money, because once they had the money and once they succeeded in building their business ventures, they would be rich and would not need Arafat any more. Whoever has the money has the power, Arafat concluded.

So the Palestinian businessmen received no money from Arafat. The money went to Arafat's personal bank accounts, to guns, bullets and terrorism. But the enterprising Palestinian businessmen decided in spite of Arafat's resistance to them, to bring their own personal fortunes accrued abroad in addition to loans taken out to build up the infrastructure anyway and they succeeded to a large extent by the summer of 2000. And this was in spite of the graft, corruption and shakedowns of these Palestinian terrorists cum Palestinian Authority.

By the summer of 2000, the Palestinian unemployment rate was as low as that in Israel – 6%. In spite of the graft and corruption of the Palestinian Authority, the economy was booming. Hotels in the Palestinian areas were full and new ones were being built just like on the Jewish side in Israel. In spite of the Palestinian terrorism and terrorists, both Israel and the Palestinians were enjoying some fruits from the Oslo Accords.

When Arafat walked out on Clinton and Barak and started his Intifada or Uprising II in September 2000, he bankrupted many of these businessmen who simply gave up and left the territories to return to the Diasporas in which they lived. Now there is virtual starvation in Gaza. The unemployment rate in Gaza since September 2000 has remained unchanged at 70% and in the West Bank (Judea and Samaria) 50%. Anarchy reins and of course, Israel is blamed, because Israel will always be blamed, but it was Arafat and his cronies who brought down this calamity on the heads of the Palestinians. All this happened because true Islam forbids true peace with Israel.

How ironic that my military commanders in the officers' course of November 1993 already knew that there never would be a Palestinian state, in spite of the signing on the White House lawn on September 13th, 1993 by Rabin, Arafat and Clinton.

In spite of Ehud Barak's sincere wish for peace and in spite of his putting "all his cards on the table," and perhaps precisely because of that, Arafat had to find a way to "pull the rug out from under everyone" and "reshuffle the deck." There could not be peace under any circumstances with Israel, even under the most generous of terms.

As a result of Intifada II, the Israeli voter booted Ehud Barak out of office and replaced him with Ariel Sharon, who during the time of the Likud being in the opposition, made best use of this time in reopening the Likud party branches that had shut down because of the bad relations between Benjamin Netanyahu and the party activists on the local level. Netanyahu left "scorched earth" in the party branches, and it was up to Ariel Sharon to "pick up the pieces" which he did well.

This prepared the way for Sharon to become prime minister in snap elections in November 2000. Sharon went on to strengthen his position in the next elections in November 2002. Again, Papa Bear Sharon gave the impression of being a strong leader, a Mr. Security if you will, just as Rabin had in 1992.

The platform of Ariel Sharon was the usual Likud platform with an emphasis on "No withdrawal from Gaza." Amram Mitzna, who replaced Ehud Barak as the new leader of the Labor Party, adopted as his central position, the immediate withdrawal from Gaza. The Likud received 40 members of Knesset out of 120 and Mitzna received 20 members of Knesset, so the people of Israel had their say, right? Wrong! As soon as Sharon formed his government with what was considered an excellent coalition of rightwing, religious and even Shinui members, he began plotting a new course: withdrawal from Gaza, precisely the election campaign plank of the Labor Party which brought about such a crushing defeat for Amram Mitzna. Sharon reversed course and hijacked the will of the majority of the people of Israel.

It seems Sharon, who was born into Socialism, became a right-winger during his military service and even played a central role in the creation of the Likud party in 1973, was now returning to his Socialist roots. The Likud party now had a Socialist leader who was ready to repeat the brutal behavior of left against the right-wingers. As had been the case in the 1940's and throughout the existence of Israel, now Sharon was going to crush the settlers in Gaza, expel them from their homes and prepare for more withdrawals from Judea and Samaria, all this, without an election or referendum to allow the people of Israel to democratically express their will. This is the tradition of Socialism.

All of a sudden, the Socialist media, bureaucrats and academics who had all cursed Sharon for decades considering him a "war criminal" were now giving him the accolades of the Savior. The settlers in Gaza and Northern Samaria were expelled from their homes in the summer of 2005 and the entire right-wing/religious population was vilified in the media, academia and the arts. It was no matter that today in Israel I believe that 70% of the population is right-wing/religious and only 30% left-wing/Socialist. But it is precisely

146

this Socialist elite of 30% which is desperately clinging to control of the government, civil service, media, and much of the economy.

There is going to be a change. There has to be a change. Indeed Benjamin Netanyahu as Finance Minister from 2003 to 2005 did a remarkable job in salvaging the shambles of Israel's shaky economy. Every time Labor is in power, the public purse is opened wide to buy the favor of the masses, to the detriment of the good of Israel's economy.

Every time the Likud returns to power, only the severest austerity measures can put Israel's economy back on track to undo the damage caused by the populism of Labor. Much more has yet to be done so that Israel will not have to look back at the difficult times of the past but to look forward to better times ahead. For this much more investment must be brought into the country. This country has to be made "user-friendly" to foreign investment, something Socialism will always thwart.

Again, Israel's population in 2006 is 7,000,000. Three million Jews more could have been here had there been employment for them. Israel's population could today have been 10,000,000.

The question is no longer whether we should be minimalist or maximalist. The 1st stage of the rocket booster, Socialism, has completed its task. Now it is time for the 2nd stage rocket to work. And this second stage is capitalism and intensive investment of people, Jews and non-Jews from all over the world.

CHAPTER SEVEN

Events Leading Up To The Creation of Israel's Bible Bloc Party

This book until now has been attempting to show the history of the three major threats facing the Jewish State today: Islam, Globalism and Socialism. The purpose of this final chapter is to provide answers to these three threats and hopefully to provide some hope for what otherwise would seem to be a hopeless situation. Whether or not people believe in God, the Bible and a Messiah from Israel who speaks Hebrew, we all know that the nature of the enemy is a religious nature, a satanic nature and openly calls for the destruction of the Jews, Christians and the entire human race. The Bible Bloc Party will speak and act clearly to counter these threats.

The situation in Israel and throughout the world is tenuous at best with disasters and catastrophes looming everywhere. My faith is that the Bible Bloc Party is part of God's plan and solution for these trying times. We can pray for God to do what WE want Him to do for us, but more importantly we must try to understand what GOD wants from us and to act accordingly.

As I complete this, my fourth book, in January 2006 at the age of 57, I look back on the trials as well as blessings that

God has bestowed on me, my family and my people Israel. As a person who believes in God, I am trying to seek out what God wants from me and from all of us. On the one hand there have been such blessings on Israel and the West, but on the other hand there are such threats and challenges from those who seek our destruction that only God's intervention can save us. Does God do this alone, or do we all have a role to play? Is it all about predestination or can we effect a change? My faith is that everything has been predestined by God, but that we do not know the plan from the beginning to the end and therefore it is upon us to act.

As it says in Ethics of the Fathers, Chapter III verses 20 & 21: Rabbi Tarfon says: The day is short, the task is abundant, the laborers are lazy, the wage is great, and the Master of the House is insistent; He used to say: You are not required to complete the task, yet you are not free to withdraw from it. In Chapter IV verse 21 it says: "Rabbi Jacob said: This world is like a lobby before the World to come; prepare yourself in the lobby so that you may enter the banquet hall."

I explained in the previous chapter about how I was fired illegally from the prime minister's office under very inauspicious circumstances. It was a Christian woman in Texas who in 1990 invited me immediately to start a new life as a lecturer in churches and synagogues in Texas and throughout the US in 1990. But by the summer of 1991, I realized that my knowledge of the Bible was insufficient for the tremendous task at hand. One cannot speak to Christians in their churches without understanding the Bible.

So, in "mid-life" crisis at age 42, I began studying to become a Conservative rabbi at the Jewish Theological Seminary in Jerusalem. For three years I was in Heaven on Earth studying God's word. They were the three happiest years of my life. Though my three years in seminary as part of the MA program prepared me for the journey I was about to embark upon as a lecturer, I was not to become a rabbi ordained by the Conservative/Masorti Movement in Israel. The reason given was: We do not feel that we can march into battle with you. You are not one of us." This means I was not a leftist like they but an avowed Likud right-winger. Out of 200 students in seminary I was the only right-winger. For a movement professing tolerance and pluralism, the Masorti/ Conservative Jewish Movement in Israel and globally has zero tolerance for the right-wing or political conservatism. Conservative Judaism is neither conservative politically or religiously. It is a left-wing oxymoron. This movement has the so-called "liberal" ideology of the left which means no toleration of the right-wing ideas or activists. Some "liberals"! In Israeli political terms, this movement is somewhere between the left-wing Labor and ultra-Left Meretz Parties.

When I was finally rejected in the third year of my MA program studies in 1994, I was asked by the board of the Seminary: "And what's this business with the Christians? Who gave you the authority to speak to the Christians?" They did not even wait for an answer. They did not want to know. Besides, these "liberals" hate the Bible believing Christians who love Israel so much.

But in answer to their question of "Who gave me the authority to speak to the Christians" I suppose the answer is "God". It was God who in His sovereignty took away my business in 1986, caused me to be fired under the most unjust circumstances from the prime minister's office in 1990, and prevented me from having a position in the IDF professional army. It was God who literally closed all the doors in my face in Israel, even in seminary, and opened the doors for me in the churches and synagogues in the US, Canada, Europe and Israel.

There was only one window of opportunity open to me. Would I in my right mind ever leave my wife, children, home and country Israel for up to eight months of the year in exile to provide for my family had a job been readily available for me in Israel? And indeed since 1990, other than the suffering caused to me and my family by my absence from home, I have been blessed in all senses of the word. But it was indeed the three years in seminary that opened my eyes to the knowledge of God's word that was so critical for me to be able to get my message through to the Christian and Jewish audiences globally.

I praise God that I was able to study these three years in seminary and hope one day to be able to return to complete my MA which was never completed because I did have to go to work to support my family. Maybe these "liberals" will be liberal enough to readmit me in the future. But after 1994, it was the churches and synagogues in which I worked that helped me to continue my education.

Indeed, my first visit to the States as a lecturer in November 1990 started out as an army spokesman's type lecture circuit warning about what was happening in the Persian Gulf as a result of Saddam Hussein's invasion of Kuwait. It did not start out as a religious message, but merely a military message.

But as the years went by, it became abundantly clear to me that what the Jews, Christians and the World were facing was a religious war. The message became a religious message for Jews and Christians. It was the same message for both. We Jews cannot survive without the Christians. The Christians cannot survive without the Jews.

When I first started speaking in 1990 fresh out of the prime minister's office, my message was received favorably in the Israeli administration and in the embassy in Washington, DC because Prime Minister Yitzhak Shamir of the Likud Party was in office.

In 1993, there was now a Labor Party government in power under Prime Minister Yitzhak Rabin, but at my IDF Spokesman's Course, I was told that there would never be a Palestinian state in spite of the Oslo Accords because the Palestinians were incapable of ruling themselves, could not provide bread and butter for their people, and finally, if they had a state, the Palestinians would be firing all kinds of missiles at us including anti-aircraft missiles, thus shutting down our airports.

So still, in the years 1992-96, I suppose it is possible to say that there was an understanding in the Israeli government for what I was doing, even though it was a Labor (Socialist) administration.

During the years 1996-99, Benjamin Netanyahu of the Likud was prime minister and I had occasion to meet with his adviser, Jonathan Brown who I know relayed my message on to the prime minister.

But in 1999 with the fall from power of Netanyahu and rise to power of Ehud Barak, there was no direct line to Barak, and I now understand why. Barak decided to "go for broke" and contrary to the very military training and life experiences I and Ehud Barak had undergone was now throwing all caution to the winds and offering Yasser Arafat 97.5% of what the Palestinians were demanding. The result was Intifada II with the deaths of thousands of innocent Israelis and Palestinians.

In 2000, Barak was out and Ariel Sharon became prime minister continuing with the same approach as Barak in spite of his election campaign promises. Israel withdrew from Gaza and four settlements in Northern Samaria, with 10,000 settlers being forcibly removed from their homes which were

153

then destroyed.

As we approach the elections of March 2006, Ariel Sharon's new political party "Kadima" promises more withdrawals from Judea and Samaria, something which defies common sense and military logic, again throwing all caution to the winds.

When I naively asked Col. Ra'anan Gissin, one of my former military commanders in the IDF Spokesman's Office and personal spokesman for Sharon to mobilize me to serve my country and government, his answer was negative. I couldn't understand him at the time. I thought that by mobilizing the Christians worldwide, I was doing the right thing for Israel. But I finally understood the thinking of the prime minister's office when Sharon said: "After we finish dealing with the Gaza settlers, we'll deal with their Christian allies as well!" So now, all of a sudden, the Christians are the enemies of Israel according to Ariel Sharon. Something is very rotten in the prime minister's office. Something is very rotten amongst the leftist Socialist leadership in Israel.

A major change had taken place in Sharon's mind to reverse course and to do exactly the opposite of what he had promised the Israelis who voted Likud. Had a referendum been held, and had the Israeli population supported the withdrawal, almost all right-wingers would have supported Sharon with all the pain. But Sharon behaved in a totalitarian, anti-democratic, Socialist manner as was his upbringing.

For years, I had seen myself as a self-appointed spokesman for Israel. Strategically, I began to understand that with so many enemies, Israel needed whatever allies it could garner. The Christians, or at least some of them, were potentially allies. These Bible-believing Christians loved Israel and the Jews and wanted to help us. Israel had to be foolhardy not to mobilize these Christians. I did not see the

154

Israeli government doing anything about it.

I will never forget when I first made aliyah (moved) to Israel in 1968 as part of the "Junior Year Program Abroad", I was interviewed by the Hebrew University student newspaper "Pi Ha'aton" and warned that the PLO was spending millions of dollars in the US and globally to tarnish Israel's image. What was Israel doing? Nothing. And nothing has really changed in all these years. The message of Israel's Foreign Ministry has always been: "Israel seeks peace, and Israel is ready to hand over territories for peace." What this really means is that Israel is guilty and must atone for all the crimes committed against the Palestinians! How absurd!

In 2003, Malcolm Hedding, Director of the International Christian Embassy of Jerusalem (ICEJ) arranged for me and my wife, Rachel, to be invited to speak to Christians in Norway and Finland.

After two weeks in Scandinavia, Rachel and I reached certain conclusions. For years, we, as Israelis, had looked at the European nations and governments as basically anti-Israel and anti-Semitic as a result of the anti-Israel decisions taken by the European Union Parliament. Europe was seen as a monolithic enemy by many of us in Israel. There was a song sung by famous Israeli singer Yehoram Gaon: "Ha'olam culo negdeinu!" (The whole world is against us.) That's the way it seems to many people in Israel as well as to Jews and Christians who love Israel.

During these two weeks in Scandinavia, the Norwegian and Finnish Christians with whom we met said to us: "You Israelis are to blame for the world being against you. We Europeans are not anti-Israel nor are we anti-Semitic. We simply are not armed with the proper information with which to defend Israel here. The negative vote of the European Union Parliament against Israel was 263 to 213. There were fifty votes more against Israel than in favor. If only the Israeli Government would send out thirty people like you and your wife to Europe for say, six months, we could reverse the negative vote. If only our representatives would hear you out, the vote could be turned into a pro-Israel vote. But your government in Israel is only capable of saying: "We apologize for the sins we have committed against the Palestinians, and for peace we are ready to withdraw from the territories of Gaza, Judea, Samaria, the Golan and even Jerusalem!" What kind of a mentally retarded foreign ministry does Israel have? Well, maybe it is not entirely retarded, but definitely Socialist and ignorant of ways in which to strategically mobilize tens if not hundreds of millions of Christians to stand with Israel in a long-haul war of religion between the Judeo-Christian West and Islam of the East.

Indeed, one of the principles of the Bible Bloc Party is to ensure that the Israeli Government establishes a board of speakers including Jews and Christians to represent Israel in Europe, the US and the rest of the world with the idea that Christians and Jews worldwide have a clear interest in standing steadfast with Israel in a war against an enemy that will never ever make true peace with Israel.

One should not think that it is a given that the Jews and Christians of the West will stand with Israel. It requires a tremendous amount of work and effort.

When I began my speaking in churches, synagogues, on radio and TV in the US in 1990, my message was merely the message of an IDF Spokesman coming to the US to talk about Desert Shield in 1990 followed by Desert Storm in 1991.

But in 1994 and after three years in Seminary studying Jewish, Christian and Islamic texts, it all of a sudden became clear to me that the Islamic war against Israel was also a war against the US, the entire Christian world and even against all of humanity. I have been dedicating the last sixteen years of my life to spreading this information, information that is buried by the media in the West and often even in Israel.

The Israeli Government lead in most part by secular people whether they are from the Labor Party or the Likud fail to understand that this is a war of religion and are therefore unable to deal with the root problem and existential threat to Israel. For them, this is a war about Palestinian rights, creating a Palestinian state, refugees, settlements, borders, Jerusalem, economics or petroleum. But it is none of these. The war is a war of religion, a war between God, God of Abraham, Isaac and Jacob, God of the Jews and Christians and Allah, the satanic god of Islam who seeks the demise of the Jews and the Christians.

At this point, I would like to discuss Egypt, one of the "brighter" sides of peace made between Israel and its Arab neighbors. What I am going to say is definitely politically incorrect and on the surface, it would seem wrong. After all, since the first visit in 1977 of former Egyptian President Anwar Sadat to Israel, we have not been at war with Egypt. That, of course, does speak for itself. But I wanted to shed some light on the goings on behind the scenes in Egypt since then which point unfortunately to Egypt preparing itself for a new war with Israel. It's only a question of the timing.

As I said at the beginning of this book, my wife, Rachel, is Egyptian born and lived the first 20 years of her life in Cairo. It was Rachel who told me on the first day we met on January 14th, 1970, that her Egyptian "friends" in school told her, "First we kill the Saturday people (the Jews) on Saturday. Then we kill the Sunday people (the Christians) on Sunday." I had always hated the Christians until I met Rachel and loved the Moslems. Rachel shattered the myth about the Moslems being our allies and the Christians the enemies.

After the assassination of Anwar Sadat by the Muslim Brotherhood extremist Islambuli in October, 1981, I called Rachel from my reserves army unit in Eilat and asked her what she thought.

Her answer was, "This is a black day for Israel. Mubarak is bad news for Israel."

My rebuttal came quickly enough, "But Prime Minister Menahem Begin likes him. President Ronald Reagan likes him. Everyone likes Mubarak. And he is committed to continuing the still fresh peace agreement between Israel and Egypt."

Rachel shattered another myth. "I know Mubarak. I grew up with him. In the 1950's and 60's, I heard him every day on the radio, saw him on TV and read his interviews in the Egyptian press. As an up and coming air force commander, he was already then being preempt for leadership in Egypt. He always said that he was the one who would one day destroy Israel. He would just do it when Egypt had prepared sufficiently and in a calculated manner. According to Rachel, Mubarak is cunning like a fox. He would attack Israel only when absolutely convinced that victory would be Egypt's."

She added, "Mark my words. There will be a war with Egypt within 20 years." (2001)

Well, the fact is Rachel was wrong about the 20 years, or was she?

I will never forget when I worked at the News Department of the Government Press Office in Jerusalem that just before Saddam Hussein's invasion of Kuwait in August 1990, my boss, then director of GPO, Dr. Yossi Olmert, came into the news room and asked me urgently to translate from Hebrew into English, what was then a secret memorandum taken out

158

of a Ba'ath Party meeting in Baghdad.

Tariq Aziz, then foreign minister of Iraq came out waving a piece of paper with the message written on it that Egypt would attack Israel two weeks after Iraq did. Now this only made sense after the Iraqi invasion of Kuwait in August, 1990 and then in January 1991 with Operation Desert Storm. Iraq launched 39 missiles at targets in Israel "hoping" that Israel would retaliate. If Israel did so, that would be the excuse for Egypt and the whole Arab world to attack Israel. So Rachel was right, Mubarak was looking for an excuse to attack Israel. But Israel did not give him that excuse. It is a fact that then US Secretary of Defense Caspar Weinberger threatened Israel with US air attack (refusal to share air codes of US fighter aircraft would bring about air battles between US and Israeli fighters over Iraq.) Israel showed restraint in spite of being attacked in an unprovoked manner by 39 Iraqi missile attacks.

So Mubarak plans for war were frustrated in 1991.

In November 1993, I participated in an IDF Spokesman's course in which we were told that Egypt was arming itself to the teeth, and yet it had no real enemies. Its neighbors: Libya, Chad and Sudan are all Arab and Muslim. There is no threat of war from them. So Egypt is arming itself for war on some other country. Guess who!

In 1995, former Egyptian War Minister Huwaidi was quoted as saying: "War with Israel is a certainty and Egypt is ready."

Egyptian War Minister Tantawi was saying: "Even though Israel has nuclear weapons, Egypt will know how to cut off the arms of the enemy when the time comes."

It must be remembered that between 1993 and 1995, Yitzhak Rabin was prime minister of Israel. In 1993, the Oslo Accords with the Palestinians were signed. In 1994, a second peace agreement with an Arab country was signed – with King Hussein of Jordan. Secret negotiations were taking place with Syria. And yet Egypt is talking of a new war with Israel... Unbelievable!

In November 1996, it was now Benjamin Netanyahu who was prime minister of Israel. I had just returned from a few months of lecture circuit in the US and received a surprise telephone call in the middle of the night from a Christian/Messianic group leader in Colorado. Normally, this gentleman would call me on a bi-weekly basis to interview me for his radio show. But this call came in the middle of the night, and it was an emergency.

With this Messianic group leader was a US Army intelligence officer with scary information. The Iraqi Army was pouring over the border from Iraq into Syria at the Abu Kamal Border crossing. The Syrians and Iraqis were about to attack Israel on the Golan Heights. Egypt was in the middle of its Badr 96 maneuvers and Saudi Arabia asked the US to turn its satellites away from certain parts of Saudi Arabia, probably from the Al Solayil oasis missile base. Built by the Communist Chinese, there were at that time 120 Dong Feng missiles, the equivalent of the US Pershing missiles, and these missiles were nuclear tipped courtesy of Abdul Kadr Khan of Pakistan. I was given code names and coordinates for all of this.

The Messianic group leader and the US Army officer made me swear that I would immediately take this to Prime Minister Benjamin Netanyahu and my immediate commander, Lt. Col. Irit Atzmon, which I did. I called Lt. Col. Atzmon in the middle of the night. She thanked me and told me to call her at any time when I received information like this.

A day passed then two then a week. No war. A week later, I

received another call. It was again from Colorado from these two men. New coordinates were given and immediately I gave them to my commander and to the prime minister's office. Again no war, praise God!

A month later, I was invited for the first and last time in my career as Israeli Army Spokesman (Reserves) to participate in war games at General Staff level. Most of the battle scenarios included the information I had submitted a month before. It included the invasion of Israel's north by Syrian and Iraqi forces and the occupation by them of the north of Israel for three days. It also included attacks from Egypt and Saudi Arabia. Again, this took place in December 1996, during the administration of Prime Minister Benjamin Netanyahu.

Jumping forward to the time of the writing of this book in 2006, we ponder the results of Egypt's recent elections. Though Mubarak maintains firm control of Egypt, the Muslim Brotherhood, once outlawed, now has about 20% of the seats in Egypt's Parliament.

Within a period of just a few weeks in late 2005, we were witnesses to the Nazi-like statements by Iranian President Ahmedinejad who said that Israel should be erased from the map, or the Al Aqsa Martyr Brigades of the PLO which said the same thing. Now the Moslem Brotherhood of Egypt is saying the same thing. The only condemnation coming out of the Islamic/Arab World was: "We should not be openly saying to Israel and World what we REALLY DO think, because this could be used against us!" But this is what all true Moslems believe. Nobody is denying that this is at the heart of their thinking.

What happens in the next general elections in Egypt? What happens if the Moslem Brotherhood wins? It means that war between Egypt and Israel is indeed inevitable.

What happens when the PLO is defeated and Hamas wins the elections in the Palestinian areas? What happens when members of the Hizbollah in Lebanon at the behest of Syria and Iran open fire on Israel with Katyusha and other rockets? And what happens when Iran goes on line with its nuclear tipped missiles? All of this means one thing: war.

For its part, Saudi Arabia has been also steadily arming itself with state-of-the-art missile technology with the aid of the Communist Chinese and the Pakistanis. This first started in 1980 when Iran was the enemy and Iraq the ally. In 1990 it was now Iraq which invaded Kuwait and thus became the enemy of Saudi Arabia and not Iran. But the fact is that Saudi Arabia today has at least 120 Chinese missiles and nuclear warheads from Pakistan.

All of these Islamic and Arab countries have only one purpose for acquiring these weaponries and that is to erase Israel from the map. The debate in Teheran has been taking place since the Ayatollah Khomeini revolution in 1979: "If we Moslems nuke Jerusalem first, Allah is God. But if the Jews and Christians nuke Mecca first, then the God of Abraham, Isaac and Jacob, the God of the Jews and Christians is God.

In January 1998, I spoke at Faith Bible Chapel in Arvada (Denver) Colorado, as part of Ted Beckett's Christian Friends of Israeli Communities conference. The purpose of this organization was to match up Jewish communities in Israel, especially in Judea, Samaria and Gaza with Christian churches in the US, Canada and the Caribbean. These churches would be expected to raise money, send volunteers and pray for the settlements.

Again it was during Prime Minister Benjamin Netanyahu's administration that President Bill Clinton forced Israel to withdraw from 80% of Hebron in February 1997. That was not all. Clinton was also forcing an Israeli withdrawal that would leave about thirty Israeli settlements isolated in the Palestinian Authority, surrounded by terrorists.

Therefore I made a speech calling for Christian ex-military volunteers from the US to come to the settlements to "Prayer Walk" alongside the Israeli guards doing their guard duty.

Obviously, American Christians would not be expected to bear arms for Israel because it would be violating federal law prohibiting US citizens from participating in foreign wars. So my call was for "Prayer walkers". But if these people had experience from the US military, and the Israeli guards took a hit from Palestinian attackers, it is fair to assume that the Christian volunteers would first attend to the Israeli guards who were now casualties, but most important of all, pick up the gun and shoot at the Palestinian attackers.

That night, Ted Beckett and I were on NBC news in Colorado Springs. The interviewer was fair and presented this issue as the first time in 2,000 years that Jews and Christians would be military allies in the Middle East! When asked by the interviewer, the response of the State Department was: "As long as this idea by Avi Lipkin remains merely hypothetical, we have no response. But we do know about Avi Lipkin and his activities!"

This plan never came to fruition also because there was a reticence by the Jewish settlers in Judea and Samaria about receiving Christian "Prayer warriors", because of the missionary aspects of the name itself.

In March 1998, two months later, I was now in Springfield, Missouri at a prophecy conference held by Dr. David Allen Lewis, one of the most pro-Israel pastors in the world. Of course, my subject was Middle East Update, but it was becoming clearer and clearer to me that President Bill Clinton was increasingly becoming a menace to Israel. Israel was being sacrificed to the Palestinians/Arabs/Moslems. The Christians were constantly asking me what they could do to help us, to help Israel.

Keeping in mind my speech two months before in Colorado calling for Christian military guards to come to Israel from the US, it all of a sudden dawned on me that now, there were many Christians serving in the Israeli military and security companies. These were the Christian spouses and relatives of Jews who had just come to Israel from the former Soviet Union and Ethiopia. God was emptying out these Diasporas and bringing home both Jews and Christians to Israel.

The Christian population in Israel had just grown from 2% Arab Christian in 1988 to a total of about 8% Christian population. Now it became 3% Arab Christian, and 5% immigrant Christians together with their Jewish nuclear families. The reason for so many Christians moving to Israel was that they were intermarried with the Jews in the former Soviet Union and Ethiopia. The Israeli Law of Return allows anyone with even only one Jewish grandparent to make Aliyah or move to Israel.

Contrary to the Arab Christians, however, the immigrant Christians served in the Israeli army just like the Jews, Druze, Circassians and some Bedouin. Those Russians who had military experience in the Soviet Army, and therefore were considered security risks in the IDF, could gain employment as private security guards at malls, restaurants, train and bus stations, etc.

Many times, when Islamic terrorists would blow themselves up, they would take with them one, two or even three guards at the entrances to the malls, train and bus stations and restaurants and hotels. Many times the dead guards were Christians.

Christians in America would ask me: How many Moslem members of Knesset are there out of a total of 120 MK's? My answer was: about 12 or 10%. How many Christian MK's were there? There were none, except, that is for Azmi Bishara, a Communist nominal Christian who didn't believe in God and was more anti-Israel than the Moslems!

The lights went on. If the Christians are about 8% of Israel population today, how can it be that there are no Bible-believing Christians in Israel's Knesset? If the majority of Israeli Moslems don't serve in the IDF and the majority of Christians do, how can it be that they pay taxes, serve in the military, and vote, and yet the Christians have no representation in Israel's legislature?

The writing was on the wall. There will be Christian members of Knesset. It was only a question of when. But then, again another question was asked. There were two possibilities. Would this party representing the Christians be a Christian party with no Jews in it? We already saw what it was like for Christians to be excluded from the Jewish parties. Perhaps the second possibility that I envision is preferable: the creation of a Judeo-Christian party with a candidate list representing the Jews and Christians equally.

We mustn't forget that 5% of Israel's population is also an immigrant population of Jews married to the Christians. Therefore the Judeo-Christian Bible Bloc would be a party with a potential constituency of 8% Christians and 5% Jews totaling 13% or 14 MK's out of 120.

And so, the idea of the Judeo-Christian Bible Bloc Party was born in March 1998 at David Allen Lewis's Prophecy Conference. Indeed, the idea was received most enthusiastically. People came up to me and asked me: When would this party be created? I answered: I don't know. I just know it's going to happen. When people pressed me,

I answered: I personally own no home in Israel and pay no taxes in Israel. I pay my income tax in the US. How can I have the "chutzpa" or nerve, audacity and gall to have any illusions of political ambition in Israel when I am a "street person" owning no home in Israel and paying no taxes?

And this was how the situation remained for six years until 2004.

Meanwhile, in 1999, my second book "Christian Revival for Israel's Survival" came out. I had seen what Clinton was doing to Netanyahu, how Israel was going to be crushed and sacrificed by US President Bill Clinton just like the Serbs in Bosnia and Kosovo. Like the Serbs, the Israelis lacked the oil, money and numbers that the Moslem backers of the Bosnians and the Albanians had. Clinton, NATO and the UN served the latter. I was desperately seeking to awaken the Christians to come to the defense of Israel, which, after all, is holy to the Christians and the Jews. Defeat for Israel, God forbid, would mean defeat for the Christians as well.

It was during my summer lecture circuit in 1999 to promote "Christian Revival" that I received one of the central testimonies to my message and especially to that of creating the Judeo-Christian Bible Bloc.

I was driving up I-5 from California to Oregon, to Washington, and then across the border to Canada. Amongst my meetings in British Columbia was what was to be a one night stand, but stretched out to three nights. It was the beginning of my nine hour seminars, three hours each over three nights.

Then I had a two day drive across the Canadian Rockies from Vancouver to Edmonton in the Province of Alberta. I arrived at a Baptist church to address almost 200 people, 12 of whom were Jews. I was honored that Jews came to the church to hear me. I spoke for four hours that night.

166

The next day was Friday, the eve of the Sabbath. My Christian hostess in Edmonton called the local Orthodox rabbi in Edmonton and arranged for me to be invited for the Sabbath at the rabbi's house. When I arrived at the synagogue just before sundown on Friday, the rabbi asked me: "So what's a nice Jewish boy like you doing in Christian churches?"

"With all due respect," I answered, "we Jews think that five million in Israel can defeat 1.3 billion Moslems plus there allies in oil corporations and banks? If we had a few tens or hundreds of millions of Christians on our side, maybe that would help level the playing field."

The rabbi begrudgingly agreed that what I was doing was correct. "I myself would never enter a church," he said, "but if you do it, I bless you."

The next day, Saturday, between the afternoon and evening services, the rabbi invited me to speak. He told the two dozen some odd congregants there that "The Christians give Avi Lipkin nine hours to speak. We will give him nine minutes!"

Within a minute or two into my presentation, there was this "knee jerk" reaction by some "left-wing liberals", and they started to heckle me and disrupt my message.

"We are not going to let you speak because you are a radical and you hate the Moslems," they said.

I answered them: "If you only knew my message, you would know that I don't hate the Moslems but love them. But they have a Nazi-like system seeking our destruction. I am only warning you of what their agenda is."

But liberals are only liberal with you when you are liberal like they. If you are not liberal like they are, they are not going to be very liberal with you! They will shout you down and not let you speak. "Left-wing liberals" are not liberals

167

at all but Socialist totalitarians whose minds are made up. Don't confuse them with the facts.

Finally, a woman stood up. She was a Christian/Messianic who attended the Jewish synagogue regularly in order to learn about Jesus the Jew. If a Christian really wants to know how Jesus prayed, preached and lived, then that Christian must go to the synagogue, because that's where Jesus prayed, preached and lived and nothing has changed in 2,000 years!

So when this woman saw me being shouted down, she offered, with my permission, of course, to share a testimony.

This lady was a social worker for the Government of Alberta, Canada. She was a case worker for a Moslem Egyptian woman doctor, who was now hiding in a safehouse in Edmonton, Canada.

Her story was terrible. In Egypt, she had a clinic and served her people, the most destitute in Egypt, much like a Mother Teresa. She was religious and attended the mosque daily. People paid her with eggs, pita bread and cheese. They did her laundry, washed her dishes and cleaned her house. But no one had money to pay her for her services.

Since she was single and in her 40's, she began to suffer from what is known in the West as "mid-life crisis." She knew that in a couple of decades, she would be too old to work and would not have any money to retire on. At least if she moved to Canada, she could accumulate a nest egg on which to retire once she reached 65 years of age.

So she applied for a visa, and it was immediately approved. The next day, there was a knock on her door. Standing at her door where three "holy" men with long beards, turbans, flowing gowns and a green Koran in each of their hands. She knew exactly who they were since she attended the mosque

168

regularly. She knew them. They knew her. So she admitted them to her home.

"Mabruk," they proclaimed. (Congratulations)

She replied "Allahi Barak Feek" (Allah should also bless you with congratulations.)

"Why do I have congratulations," she asked.

"Because we know you're going to Canada."

"Well how did you know that? That was just approved yesterday."

They answered her. "We know everything about you. We have our people everywhere in the Egyptian Government administration. And yes, we also have congratulations in store for us as well."

"Why?" she asked.

"You are going to work for us. You are going to be our spy in Canada."

"What does that mean?"

"As a doctor with a clinic, you will be in a position to know who the Jews and Christians are in Edmonton. Your fame precedes you. You will be one of the most popular doctors in Edmonton. Jews and Christians will come seeking your services in addition to the Moslems. The law requires these patients to fill out comprehensive forms with all their private data. You will know where the Jews live, where they work, their telephone numbers, emails, and social security numbers. You will know where to find them at any given moment. You will provide this information to us.

When the "big" war breaks out in the Middle East, we will kill them all. And all those Christians who are married to the Jews and the children of these intermarriages must also be killed. And the pastors of Christian and Messianic congregations that love Israel must all be targeted as well."

This woman doctor was taken aback. She replied: "You

men know that I attend the mosque regularly, pray five times a day as a true Moslem, give Zaqat (charity) and am loyal to Allah. But I am also a doctor who swore the Hippocratic Oath to feed the people and save lives. I don't understand politics. I am not interested in politics. And I am definitely not into killing people, Jews or otherwise."

"So you're not going to work for us, right?"

"That's right," she said.

"OK" was their response.

Now, standing next to this doctor was a woman, her best friend and helper at her clinic. These three "holy" men grabbed the friend, pulled out a knife and slit her throat.

The woman lay there dying, and they said to her: "If you don't work for us, that's what we're going to do to you!"

The next day, Praise God, this woman doctor received political asylum at the Canadian Embassy in Cairo, Egypt and the Royal Canadian Air Force flew in a private jet to pick her up and frisk her away to a hiding place in Canada.

And this Messianic woman at the Jewish synagogue gave me a testimony that was more important for me and my message than had I spoken. God had a reason for me to drive across the Canadian Rockies, to be silenced and to listen to this shocking testimony.

The Messianic woman continued and said: "According to the RCMP (Royal Canadian Mounted Police) 90% of the Moslems in Canada are good people. They are law abiding, peaceful people. But 10% of these people get their salaries from the mosques and their orders from the Middle East. The 10% know the agenda.

When a war breaks out in the Middle East, these Moslems will know where to find the Jews and certain Christians. The Moslems of Edmonton will kill the Jews of Edmonton. The Moslems of Vancouver will kill the Jews of Vancouver, etc.

170

We are already witness in 2005 to the riots and massacres in France that the Moslems are carrying out against the Jews there. The Moslems, in each and every Western community in the world know where to find the Jews and the Christians who are with the Jews. I believe this is so also in the United States and in South America.

Just as the fig tree has the former fruits in the spring and the latter fruits (the bumper crop in the fall) so, too, have the Jews of the former Soviet Union been the former fruits and the Jews of the West will be the latter fruits who will either be massacred by the Moslems everywhere, or they will flee to Israel.

The Jews in Israel are now about five million. But there are about another ten million Jews scattered throughout the world. Since intermarriage rates are about 50 to 70%, it really means that between fifteen and twenty million people, Jews and their Christian spouses and the children of these intermarriages are candidates to move to Israel when a war breaks out in the Middle East and orders are given to massacre the Jews everywhere. Again, this is part and parcel of Islam to kill the Jews on Saturday and the Christians on Sunday.

What I have been attempting to do in this book is to show that a war is inevitable in the Middle East. This will be followed inevitably by a massacre of Jews and Christians throughout the world which will spark a massive "tsunami" of millions of Jews and Christians who will move to Israel.

Again, the debate among Islamic theologians in Iran is that if they nuke Jerusalem first, their god, Allah is God. They pray "Allahu Akbar" or Allah is greater than the God of the Jews and Christians. If Jerusalem is nuked, there will be no Messiah on the Mt. of Olives, first or second coming. That proves that the Bible is a pack of lies.

171

That proves that the Koran is the true book and Islam is the true religion.

But conversely, if Mecca is nuked by the Jews and Christians, their god Allah has turned out to be a lesser god, a liar and cheater. They will all then convert to faith in the God of Abraham, Isaac and Jacob.

This psychosis known as Islam will not stop until it is stopped, so a war is inevitable. A massacre of Jews and Christians is then inevitable. A mass immigration to Israel is inevitable. When that happens, any political party representing both Jews and Christians will be thrust into the limelight as Israel's largest political party representing Israel's largest constituency: the Jews and the Christians who will be coming home with their Jewish spouses and blood relatives.

This is the end time scenario as I see it. The coming of the Messiah will be directly connected to the millions of Jews and Christians coming home to Israel on that day.

CHAPTER EIGHT

The Formation of Israel's Bible Bloc Party

As I said in the previous chapter, I had been promoting the idea of a Judeo-Christian political party to run for Israeli Knesset elections for six years without having any idea of how and when this party would be formed.

Without boring the reader with too many details of my earlier life, again, I must reemphasize that by 1986, God had taken away my business, my home, the wealth I brought from the US as an immigrant, my car and virtually all my worldly possessions in Israel. But God did leave me my wife, my children, my health and a desire to serve Him.

It reminds me of the Frank Sinatra song: "I want to do it my way!" So, I feel that God was saying to me: "Avi, I want you to do it my way!"

I was fired illegally from the prime minister's office, blacklisted in the civil service in Israel, and could not get ordination in the Conservative/Masorti Movement of Israel and all the doors, it seemed were slammed hermetically shut in my face in Israel.

It was Nancy, a Christian woman in Texas who in 1990 showed me that God's plan was to open up many of the doors in the Christian world to a Jew from Israel who could

173

come and tell them things as they really were, to call a spade a spade.

I was a Jew who overcame my hatred of the Christians and fell in love with them understanding that Christians (at least some of them) are not Israel's best friends but Israel's only friends. By the way, I never stopped loving the Moslems, the Arabs, or the Palestinians as human beings.

I worked myself to the limit to write my first book in 1997, then a second in 1999, a third in 2003 and now my fourth book in 2006. I have a website with a bookstore that sells these books along with my first book in German. I now also offer audio tapes, videos, CD's and DVD's of one, three and ten hour teachings.

I had to work very hard to produce these teaching resources and am pleased they are now blessing people around the world. God is definitely blessing me!

Thanks to these products selling and to my family's sacrificing to allow me to travel worldwide for up to eight months per year, I was able to marry off my two sons to the most wonderful daughters-in-law in the world and to help to provide for them along with my in-laws for a roof over their heads.

And yet in the summer of 2004, after almost twenty years of renting a home in what it would seem to be an endless process, my wife and I were still theoretically "homeless" in the sense that we had no permanent home. We were always renting and moving every few years, whenever our landlord decided to sell his property, thus forcing us to look for a new rented home.

I had sworn to God and to the Christians that if/when God provided us with a home, and when God had me paying income taxes in Israel in addition to the United States, then that would be a sign to form the Judeo-Christian political party I had been talking about for six years.

It was at the end of July 2004 that I was completing a lecture circuit of a few months and was on my last day of driving eastward back to New York to catch my EL AL flight back to Israel. My cell phone rang as I was driving. It was Rachel. Now, of course, you understand, I was always happy when Rachel called me, especially so at the end of this very successful lecture tour. I was only a few days away from home and missed Rachel so much.

But she had some distressing news for me. Our landlord had just sold the home we had been renting for four years, and Rachel was trying to negotiate an extension of a month or two to allow us more time to find a suitable accommodation.

Indeed the same thing happened to us four years before. On the very day my first grandchild was born, our previous landlord also gave us marching orders. But that very same night in August 2000 we miraculously found this wonderful place to rent that lasted us until July 2004. So I thought that again, God would miraculously find us a flat or house to rent in a day or a few days.

But I was angry. Here I was working so hard for God. God has us kicked out of our home. "Why, God? Why are you doing this do us? You know that I have promised You that when I have the money, I will buy the right home, and then we move."

But from my short life's experience, I see that God does not necessary and usually does not work in a way that we expect or want. God works in His own way, and we have to learn to "get over it." Years later, we realize that God's plan had a reason, and it was for the better. Without any real finances, we were about to be blessed by God with a home.

Indeed, my wife and I searched for four months, including all of September, October, November and most of December.

We looked at over 100 homes and apartments in at least 12 neighborhoods of Jerusalem and its surroundings. What I liked, my dear wife hated and vice versa. We averaged almost three homes a day, with our landlord's patience running out. The insecurity of not knowing where we were going to live tormented us.

Most important of all, we had only $12,000 in our hands. Now for anyone who knows the Israeli real estate market, $12,000 will not buy very much, not in Israel nor really anywhere else.

A fairly decent four-room apartment in Israel goes for about $250,000. Mortgage banks provide for anywhere between 50-70% of the financing, but we needed to come up with the balance.

We came to the settlement of Kedar in the Judean Desert. This "settlement" in "the territories" has a "build your own home" system. We first had to be accepted by the membership committee, which we were and then had to pay $28,500 membership fee.

The contractor would then build a house according to the standard plans of the homes in Kedar. With the adding of a third floor (as a lecture room/office), the price was about $232,000. The total came out $270,000 without embellishments.

So of our $12,000 in hand, $10,000 went to the Kedar membership fee, and $2,000 to the contractor.

We are now a year after the signing. The house is virtually complete and our mortgage bank provided 70% of the funding. The rest came from hard work in the US, Canada and Europe. Of course, Rachel's work at the Israeli Radio Service for the last 25 years made its mark as well.

So God was good to us. We should be moved into our new house by May 2006. Now that I own a home in Israel, I am no longer homeless. My first precondition for starting the party has been met.

As for paying income taxes, I had already been paying income taxes in the US since 1990 (when I left the prime minister's office in Israel) because all my income was in the US, and not a penny from Israel. I just rested in Israel with my family between lecture circuits abroad.

But thanks to an economic reform bill by then Israel's Finance Minister Benjamin Netanyahu in 1993, I was now required from 2003 to report to the Israeli IRS as well. Even though I was making all my income abroad, this new law required Israelis for whom Israel was the "center of their lives" to pay a differential tax to Israel in addition to the taxes paid abroad.

So now, I am in the process of paying my 2003, 2004, 2005 and 2006 taxes in Israel all at the same time and in addition to the already paid taxes in the US! God has provided for that as well.

So the second precondition for forming the party has been met.

And so it was that in January 2005, I met with Advocate Calev Myers of the Yehuda Raveh law firm in Jerusalem, in order to turn this "pipedream" of six years into a reality. It is no longer a pipedream. The party is now in its embryonic stage.

The Knesset Elections Committee has established that for a political party to be registered and recognized by the Knesset three things must be submitted: At least three of the party's principles, at least 100 signatures of Israeli citizens and finally a registration fee of about $16,000. This is in addition to the lawyer's fee of $15,000 for 100 hours of work. (Calev has already been paid $5,000 as of January 2006.)

So I prepared eight principles. Calev Myers prepared the

by-laws of the party. And I began mobilizing funds abroad which is allowed until the party is recognized. After the party is recognized, no more funds from abroad are allowed. Only funds from Israeli voters will be accepted. Calev and I began collecting the first founders' signatures out of the hundred founders of the party.

The following are the eight principles:

1. The Gush Hatanakhi/Bible Bloc Party bases its principles on the ethics and teachings of the Bible, the God of Abraham, Isaac and Jacob, and faith in the coming of the Messiah who is a Jew from Israel who speaks Hebrew.

2. The Gush Hatanakhi Party stands for the integrity of the Land of Israel as the Jewish State based on the promises of the Bible. The Gush Hatanakhi Party opposes any further withdrawals after the tragedy of the withdrawal from Gaza and northern Samaria.

3. The Gush Hatanakhi Party stands for the defense of all those who believe in the Bible and opposes the ethnic cleansing of Jews and Christians from the entire Land of Israel. This includes the ethnic cleansings of Christians from Arabic speaking areas and Jews from Gaza, Judea, Samaria and the Golan.

4. The Gush Hatanakhi Party understands the threat facing Israel and the civilized world from Islamo-Fascist terrorism and will work to unite all enlightened forces in Israel and globally to defeat Islamo-Fascism. A Bible Bloc International representing all Judeo-Christian Western Civilization and Democracy

political parties will be established in Jerusalem for this purpose.

5. The Gush Hatanakhi Party will endeavor to strengthen Israel by creating a real public relations agenda providing speakers, both Jewish and Christian to mobilize support for the State of Israel and for the defense of Judeo-Christian Western Civilization and Democracy.

6. The Gush Hatanakhi Party will endeavor to strengthen Israel by attracting investors from all over the world, especially Jews and Christians, to invest in Israel and expand Israel's truncated economic infrastructure something which frustrates immigration and encourages emigration.

7. The Gush Hatanakhi Party views the exodus or "yerida" of over 3 million Jews from Israel over the last 57 years as a national tragedy that must and can be corrected. An improved and expanded economic infrastructure will serve this purpose.

8. The Gush Hatanakhi Party will endeavor to thwart Islamo-Fascism plans for the shedding of blood of Jews and Christians in the Diaspora by Islamic terrorism, and hopes to create ways and means of absorbing victims of such terrorism as new immigrants into Israel as a solution for Jews and Christians who will flee to Israel during these trying times.

As for the mobilization of funds from abroad, there are a handful of people who are helping to raise the funds. These dear Christians are not rich people. But their money is very

179

dear to me precisely because they are not rich. They are like the widow giving her last mite!

But throughout the sixteen years of my work in churches in synagogues, it has always been the poorest and not the richest who gave so generously for me to continue my work of lecturing, writing books, creating educational resources, and now building my home, paying my taxes both in the US and Israel, and finally creating the Bible Bloc Party.

As for the signatures, we have only just begun. We have the 100 signatures assured to us as soon as the March 28th, 2006 Israeli elections are over. Many people wanted to sign now, before the elections, but felt it would not be ethical to be founders of one party and to vote for another. I concurred, so as this book is being printed, I am in the US again for another two month lecture circuit cum fundraiser for the party and hope that all the monies and signatures will be accumulated to register the party with the Israeli Knesset Elections Committee.

We then have to be approved by this committee. That also takes about six weeks.

Theoretically, the next elections in Israel after March 28th 2006 are scheduled for four years later or 2010. But with the vicissitudes of Israel's politics, the next elections could be three years away, two, one, or even six months away if the Israeli Government falls in a no-confidence vote by a majority of 61 out of 120 MK's.

There are two ways in which the party will become known to the Israeli public. One way is the quiet way or under the radar. As I am writing this chapter, Israeli Prime Minister Ariel Sharon is lying in Hadassah Hospital in Jerusalem incapacitated due to massive bleeding in the brain brought on by certain medications he was taking after a minor stroke in December 2005.

American Christian Evangelist and leader Pat Robertson is being vilified in the Israeli press for saying basically that if God says in the Bible not to divide up the Land of Israel and an Israeli leader transgresses God's word by dividing His land, then if that leaders becomes ill, maybe its divine punishment. Atheists and Socialists cannot bear to hear preaching like this.

I recently spoke before a convention of Christian women in Jerusalem (Women on the Wall) of Evangelist Christine Darg, and quoted Psalm 137: "If I forget thee, Oh, Jerusalem, let my right hand forget its cunning. Let my tongue cleave to my palate if I don't place you (Jerusalem) above all my joys."

How does one medically describe the right hand forgetting its cunning or the tongue cleaving to its palate? I believe the condition is known as a stroke or cerebral hemorrhage which is exactly what Sharon is suffering from. Sharon and his henchmen are planning to divide up not only Judea and Samaria, but Jerusalem as well. One has to be completely blind, deaf and dumb not to see God's work in action here.

As much as we mourn for Yitzhak Rabin being assassinated, how can we not see that that what felled Ariel Sharon was not the assassin's bullet, but God's hand in the form of stroke and then cerebral hemorrhage? We love Ariel, the man, the Jew. We love Ariel Sharon, Israel's war hero, general, and creator of the settlements. But Prime Minister Ariel Sharon divided the land, uprooted 10,000 Jewish settlers from their homes, with many of them still waiting for alternative homes and employment. And he's planning to do it again in Judea and Samaria with no peace in exchange. There was no assassin here as in the case of Rabin. Strokes and cerebral hemorrhages are from God. Smell the coffee.

Of course, if one doesn't believe in God, God forbid, all

181

of this is preposterous, but if we don't believe in God and the Bible, then there is no justification for a Jewish state in the Land of Israel. It is all based on God's word the Bible. And that's the reason for this party. True Jews and Christians believe in God's word, the Bible, and in Israel's right to existence as the fulfillment of God's word.

If I apologize for what I have just said, as Pat Robertson is being pressured to do, I am basically denying the veracity of the Bible.

The second way of promoting Israel's Bible Bloc is via the media. But if I decide to promote this party through the newspapers, radio and TV, I already know I will be vilified as well. So the first stage of creating this party will be low key, based on individuals and individual groups of people in their homes and meeting places.

I speak fluent Russian and Arabic and will be meeting with the primary constituents who potentially will be voting for this party: Russian and Arabic speakers.

My idea had originally been that we would participate in these elections on March 28th 2006 which were to have originally taken place in November 2006. But with basically only three months to prepare for the earlier date, there was not enough time to meet the voters and choose the candidates. Again, many people could not or would not support the Bible Bloc because they did not want to split up the right-wing vote to prevent any further dividing of the land. I understand that and respect that.

So the party's 100 founders will be mobilized after the elections in March 2006.

My prediction is that I will travel the country from north to south and from east to west to meet as many people as possible in a never ending process until the next elections after 2006.

Inevitably, we will be on the radar screens of the leftist media and establishment that at first will not take the Bible Bloc or me seriously, but later will vilify me as this party takes root. It will also vilify those who march with me, because these people in the media and government have no room in their hearts for God and do not understand that the war with the Moslems is a war with Satan. It is a war between God and Satan. Those people who have no conception of God cannot have a conception of Satan and those who follow him, the Moslems. It is only people led by God who can defeat people led by Satan.

My prediction is that the Bible Bloc has a potential constituency at this moment of anywhere between 10 -15 MK's making it one of Israel's biggest political parties and definitely a swing-vote party as part of a right-wing religious coalition.

As part of the eight principles, the Bible Bloc would be dedicated to fulfilling an economic plan I presented to the Israeli government in 1986, but was never answered. The Israeli Government will endeavor to carry out a census of Jews and Christians throughout the Diaspora who will be committed to bring their wealth and expertise to provide for investments and infrastructure throughout Israel. When this is done, there will be no more unemployment in Israel. Israel must prepare an infrastructure of employment for up to twenty million people, Jews and their Christian spouses and relatives who will be coming home to the Land of Israel when the Moslems go on the rampage to annihilate the "Jews on Saturday and Christians on Sunday."

It is the purpose of this party to see the writing on the wall and to act accordingly.

The Knesset candidate list will have 50% Jewish candidates (slots 1, 3, 5, 7, 9, etc.) and 50% Christian candidates (slots 2,

4, 6, 8, 10, etc.). The Christian candidates will include Arabic speaking Christians, Russians, Ukrainians, Ethiopians and born-again Westerners.

The Jewish list will include Orthodox, Conservative, Reform and secular Jews. Women candidates will be sought out to run from both Christian and Jewish lists.

Hopefully, except for rare occasions, it is the intention of the Bible Bloc Party to field candidates who served in the IDF.

Other principles of the party not amongst the eight primary principles are recognition of the Armenian Holocaust in WWI, opposition to homosexuality, pornography, abortion and paganism of all sorts, as based on Bible principles.

Israel's Bible Bloc will work towards the end of creating a Bible Bloc International in which all political parties and organizations of all countries in the world that subscribe to the principles of the Bible will open offices in Jerusalem much like Communist parties did in Moscow as part of the Communist International or Socialist parties in Vienna as part of the Socialist International.

It cannot be otherwise, because the Bible is the #1 best-seller in human history. It is the book of God, the book on which Western Civilization and Democracy are based and from which all our modern blessings are derived. To defend the Bible is defend human civilization.

184

CHAPTER NINE

The Bible Bloc International

My third book, "Islamic Threat Updates Almanac #1 5762" came out in March 2003 though it is based on the events immediately following the aftermath of the 9/11 attacks in the US from October 2001 to September 2002.

I hope that after the publishing of this fourth book: "Israel's Bible Bloc" I will be able to return to the information I have accumulated from October 2002 to September 2003 and produce my fifth book: "Islamic Threat Updates Almanac #2 – 5763" and so forth and so on for each year since then.

But there are some indeed pertinent facts and experiences that I experienced in Greece in 2001 and since the writing of my third book which need to be included in this ninth and final chapter of this book. It is this very information I received, especially during my travels in Europe that brought me to the conclusion that a "Bible Bloc International" must be created in Jerusalem to represent Christian and conservative parties worldwide in our joint battle to save Judeo-Christian Western Civilization and Democracy which is now under attack from Islam.

In April and in August of 2001, I had the opportunity to be invited to speak in Athens, Greece to some born-again

Christians. I was told that the Greek population totaled about 10 million people most of all of them Greek Orthodox Christians. But the Socialist PASOK government had given asylum as a humanitarian gesture to half a million Albanian Moslems to come live in Greece.

So now Greece's population became 5% Moslems plus another 1% Turks from Thrace in the eastern part of Greece bordering on Turkey and Bulgaria. Thus the total Islamic population in Greece now was 6%. Since the Moslems have up to ten children per family and the Greeks average just two children, the Moslems may soon become a sizeable minority and if unchecked, could become the majority in Greece. When that happens, there would be a solid Islamic land bridge from the Bosporus all the way to the Adriatic Sea, including Albania, Kosovo, Bosnia and soon Macedonia.

My Greek hosts also told me that in 1923 during the terrible war with Turkey which the Greeks lost under General Venizelos, the Turkish population then was ten million and the Greek population was ten million. Eighty years later. The Turkish population has mushroomed to seventy million and the Greeks remain at the same ten million. All Greeks were expelled from Anatolia. It is hard to believe that the seven original churches of Christianity are in what is today Turkey, but that there are no more Christians in Turkey, which for a thousand years was the Byzantine Empire. I think it's called ethnic cleansing.

The Moslems are winning in the Balkans and Southeastern Europe by demography. And the Socialist government under PASOK actually goes and invites hundreds of thousands of Moslems to come to live in Greece thus threatening the Christian and Western character of Greece. Not only is the Socialist leadership of Israel stupid.

In July 2002, Rachel and I had the honor of being invited

186

by ICEJ Director Malcolm Hedding to travel with him to speak in Hamar, Norway and then to continue on to speak in six cities in Finland with Ulla Jarvilehto, director of the local branch of the ICEJ in Finland.

Our overwhelming experience from this trip was that Israel's PR campaign is non-existent. The Israeli Foreign Ministry is not doing its job, which is to convince the world and in this case Scandinavia of the rightness of Israel's positions. Instead the Israel Foreign Ministry only says, "We want peace. We are ready to do almost anything for peace. All our sins against the Palestinians will be atoned for!"

This approach, which has always been the approach of the Foreign Ministry in Jerusalem is Socialist. It is defeatist and a non-starter. It will not gain friends for Israel's cause.

It was at about this time that the European Union Parliament voted against Israel by 263 against Israel to 213 in favor of Israel on some question or other. In Israel, the media cried the usual "Woe is me" and that the whole world was against us, that there was nothing that could be done, that the Europeans are anti-Semites and anti-Israel.

Well, after two weeks in Scandinavia, my wife and I came away with quite a different conclusion. We were told in no uncertain terms that Israel's PR debacle was Israel's fault, not because of Israel's position toward the peace process or European anti-Semitism but because Europeans were not getting the truth in their local media outlets, which were controlled by money. It was the Islamic petrodollar and the globalist agenda which controlled the media. The Israeli government was doing nothing to remedy the situation.

The Norwegian and Finnish Christians told us that if Israel would send another thirty spokespersons like myself and my wife, that we could convince a few dozen deputies in the European Union Parliament to switch their votes in favor of Israel. It could be done if Israel only decided to do it. If only 25 deputies switched over in favor of Israel, the vote would be tied. And if 26 deputies switched over, Israel would have a pro-Israel vote in the European Parliament 239 to 237. It was not an impossible task. All Israel needed was the resolution to reach out with an information offensive to the deputies and to reach out to the public in Europe in general and Scandinavia in particular.

But alas, as I mentioned earlier, the Israeli Foreign Ministry, as is all the civil service controlled by the Socialists, is inept, corrupt, and therefore doomed to failure.

Therefore, one of the principles of the Israel Bible Bloc Party is the creation of a speakers' bureau including Jewish and Christian speakers throughout Europe and the world to get the justice of Israel's message out to all nations.

All this was mentioned earlier in this book, but now I take this one dimension further. If all right-wing, Christian and conservative political parties would only open up an office branch in Jerusalem, as part of an overall strategy of unity to defend our common values throughout the world, this, too, would strengthen Israel's position in the debates which take place in the European Union's Parliament. The parties that would have liaison offices in Israel would thereby become de facto ambassadors for Israel in Europe. Maybe Bible Bloc parties should be created worldwide in each country for this purpose.

I don't accept the notion that Europe is anti-Semitic, anti-Israel and monolithic. Europe can be pro-Israel if Israel decides to roll up its sleeves and reach out to the Europeans. And when the Europeans see that Jerusalem has offices for political parties from all over the Western World, it will show the love that Israel really does have for our Christian brethren in Europe and in the West.

In January 2003, I was again honored by ICEJ Director Malcolm Hedding to travel for some more lectures to Norway, this time in Oslo. I was called at the last moment to replace an important lecturer from Jerusalem who at the last minute could not make the trip.

Again, this was a trip which included a high-level meeting with the prime minister of Norway as well as members of the Norwegian parliament from many parties, all of whom were pro-Israel. Except for the Israeli ambassador, there was no participation from other people from Israel or from the local Oslo Jewish community. What a pity! There is so much that can be done and is not being done.

In September 2003, Rachel and I were invited to speak in Switzerland by the Pro-Israel Christian group based in Thun. Werner Scherer, our host, had us appear in seven German speaking cities. Because these meetings were political, they were held in public meeting places, not in churches. Because these meetings were open to the public, many Moslems living in Switzerland came to hear me.

It was during these meetings that some journalists from the Arab World came to hear me speak. As a result I made first page of such newspapers of "AL WATAN", the biggest newspaper in Saudi Arabia and "AL SHARQ AL AUSAT", the biggest Arabic language newspaper in the world published in London. In both newspapers I was described as a senior Mossad official sent by Jerusalem to mobilize the Christians to support Israel. I wish it were true! I wish I were Mossad. I wish I was sent by Jerusalem. But the fact is that what I do is done at my own initiative, expense and at the risk of my life! But it is true that I am working tirelessly to mobilize the Christians for Israel.

Interestingly, the most interesting part of the lectures was at the end when the Moslems would come up to confront me

189

and Rachel in debate in Arabic. They tried to intimidate us.

Luckily unlike Dutch artist and movie maker Theo van Gogh, we were not assassinated by them.

They said to my wife: "The Europeans colonized us Moslems for centuries. Now it's our turn to colonize the Europeans! Victory will be ours by Allah."

My wife asked them: "Why did you leave Egypt?"

The Egyptian answered: "There's no work in Egypt. There's no democracy in Egypt."

My wife countered: "And that's exactly what you want to bring to Europe: an Islamic takeover that would destroy the very European Christians who blessed you Moslem immigrants with freedom, democracy and employment."

In October 2003, I visited Holland for the first time as a speaker. My Christian hosts took me to speak in The Hague as part of a brief stop on my way to New York.

On my return trip to Israel via Amsterdam, I again stopped in The Hague and then in Echten for a mini-lecture circuit in Holland. I also visited Antwerp, Belgium, for the first time and met with Philippe de Winter, head of the nationalist Flemish Blok Party of Belgium.

It is interesting to see how the Flemish Blok was actually pro-Nazi during WWII, but in the last two decades has realized its error and reversed course. This party is now pro-Israel, pro-Jewish and pro-Zionist. While the Moslems are threatening to kill the Jews in Belgium, it is the Flemish Blok now renamed Flemish Belange that makes every effort to defend the Jews, especially in Antwerp, the economic hub of the Flemish part of Belgium.

Both Holland and Belgium suffer from out of control Islamic demographic growth. Official estimates in Holland are that there are one million Moslems there. Unofficial estimates are that there are two million Moslems or 16% of the population. Like Greece, the Europeans have one or two children per family while the Moslems have close to ten children. There are great fears in both countries that Islam will take over within thirty years.

In March 2004, I spoke before the Flemish Blok Party in Antwerp. Interestingly the Dutch speaking Protestants of Holland decided to "boycott" me ever since because the Dutch are Protestants and the Flemish of Belgium are Dutch Catholics. It seems the Wars of Reformation are not yet over. I told the Dutch Protestants that they need to "get over it" already. If the Catholics and Protestants in Europe don't work together, the Moslems win in Holland and Belgium.

Also in March 2004, Rachel and I took a long needed vacation on the southern coast of Spain near Malaga. I already explained earlier in this book about how Islam ruled Spain for close to 800 years and plans to return again to rule Spain. Out of a population of forty million Spaniards, officially one million are Moslems, mostly immigrants from North Africa.

The approach of the Spanish government as well as throughout Western Europe is that the Moslems are needed to fill the ranks of the depleted European Christians in the labor market. Since WWII, the Europeans have been seeking to create welfare states. Families bore only one or two children and yet retirement and welfare benefits skyrocketed. In order to pay for that, "new blood" was necessary, and so the Moslem and African laborers were invited into Europe to keep the economy afloat. That is one reason the Moslems are "untouchable" in Europe. No one may dare criticize them. They are too needed for the Europeans to maintain their standard of living and comfort levels.

Secondly, I think that the riots that took place in France in the fall of 2005 are another reason no Christian/European politicians want to deal with the cancerous growth of the Moslem communities in Europe. Any sign of anti-Arab or anti-Islamic policies will spark "Intifadas" or uprisings all over Europe. These uprisings will destroy the European economies. They will also signal the end of the European comfort zones.

Rachel and I also had an interesting excursion to the British colony of Gibraltar at the southern tip of Spain. While looking for a parking space for our rented car, we noticed we were just outside of one of Gibraltar's newspapers. When a gentleman emerged from the newspaper offices, I approached him to ask if he was driving away with his car leaving us his parking space. He answered in the negative.

Then I asked him a couple of questions:

What was the population of Gibraltar? He answered that the population totaled 28,000 people.

He saw I was Jewish, so I asked how many Jews were there in Gibraltar. He answered that there were 600 Jews (2.3%) Hindus 500 (2%) and Moslems 7,000 or (25%).

Again, given the fact that Moslems can freely immigrate to Gibraltar from anywhere in the British Commonwealth and given the fact that they out-produce the non-Moslems demographically, if Spain does not retake the territory of Gibraltar from the liberal English, the Moslems will eventually become the majority in Gibraltar, Gibraltar (Jebel Tariq in Arabic) will declare its independence and become an Islamic republic in one of the most strategic areas of the world.

The mosque we saw at the very tip of the colony was dedicated by Saudi Arabia and King Fahd for that very purpose!

So Spain is being invaded again by Islam and has forgotten the 800 years of "reconquista" or re-conquest. King Ferdinand and Queen Isabela: Where are you when we need you?!

England reputedly has more mosques now than churches.

According to the Egyptian magazine AL-Mussawar, Lady Diana was reported to have converted to Islam and was bearing Dodi Fayed's child before her assassination by MI6. Can you imagine the mother of the future King of England being a Moslem? Can you imagine that the half brothers and half sisters of the King of England, Defender of the Anglican Church being Moslems? Even Prince Charles is pro-Moslem.

Austria's population is now 30%. At this rate, in thirty years, Austria will be a Moslem country. What the Turks could not achieve in 200 years at the gates of Vienna, the Moslem immigrants are doing by producing Moslem babies and a continued influx of migrant workers. And just as a drug addict cannot live without his fix, so, too, can the Europeans not live without their Moslem laborers who keep their economies floating.

And if anyone tries to talk about this in Europe, they will be arrested and tried for "hate crimes." The right-wing, conservative and Christian parties are too afraid to break that law and speak about this. The Flemish Blok in Belgium was banned by a French judge in Ghent and had to reform under the new name Flemish Belange. The Jews are living on their suitcases ready to flee Europe because another Holocaust is coming. But this time, the Holocaust is not from the Christians but from the Moslems. The Christians in Europe have not awakened yet. In fact, many Europeans in their fantasy have converted to Islam and joined the sickness known as Islam.

I will not forget that when Italian Foreign Minister Gianfranco Fini visited Israel recently, he said in a press conference with Prime Minister Ariel Sharon that the terrorist who blew himself up killing 21 Italian policemen in Iraq in May 2003 was an Italian himself who had converted to Islam in Italy and then was sent as a "reporter" to Iraq by Al Qaeda purportedly to interview his fellow countrymen serving in Iraq and when he sat down to have lunch with them, blew himself up. Is that not a psychosis?

So the Moslems even take Christians, brainwash them, convert them to Islam and then use them as ticking time bombs to kill their fellow countrymen.

And of course, Jewish and Christian women are fair game for Moslem men who charm their victims, marry them, force them to convert to Islam and become baby factories for Allah's Jihad.

The purpose of the Bible Bloc International in Jerusalem, Israel will be two-fold: to strengthen Israel's position internationally with the solidarity of those Western countries' parties that open offices in Jerusalem as part of the this plan, and secondly to strengthen the Christian countries of the West with a central organization in Jerusalem sending out a clear message needed to preserve Judeo-Christian Western Civilization and Democracy worldwide.

Israel's Bible Bloc Party will be responsible for hosting the Bible Bloc International and will ensure a good welcome and hospitality to all Jews and Christians "coming home" to the Holy Land.

When Jews and Christians will love each other and be united in the Land, then maybe, just maybe, God will be pleased enough with all of us to finally defeat Islam. Either we "hang together" or hang separately.

When the Jews and Christians can learn to love each other, maybe only then will we deserve that God send the Messiah because we shall then have proven to Him that we have fully absorbed the meaning of "Love the Lord thy God" and "Love thy neighbor as thyself". Only then with the final defeat of Islam during the messianic era will there be peace on Earth.